D1286027

THE STORY OF

TWAS THE NIGHT
BEFORE CHRISTMAS

Clement Clarke Moore (1779–1863)
Portrait painted late in life for the General Theological Seminary

THE STORY OF

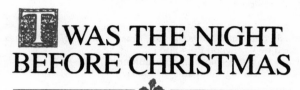

'TWAS THE NIGHT BEFORE CHRISTMAS

GERARD & PATRICIA DEL RE

PELICAN PUBLISHING COMPANY
Gretna 2001

Copyright © 1991
By Gerard Del Re
All rights reserved

Previously published under the title *'Twas the Night Before Christmas*
Published by Wynwood Press, 1991
Published by arrangement with the author by
  Pelican Publishing Company, Inc., 2001

No part of this publication may be reproduced, stored in a retrieval system, or transmitted in any form or by any means—electronic, mechanical, photocopy, recording, or any other—without the prior written permission of the publisher. The only exception is brief quotations in printed reviews.

Library of Congress Cataloging-in-Publication Data

Del Re, Gerard, 1944-
    The story of 'twas the night before Christmas : the life and
times of Clement Clarke Moore and his best-loved poem of
yuletide / Gerard and Patricia Del Re.
      p. cm.
    ISBN 1-56554-914-7
    1. Moore, Clement Clarke, 1779-1863. Night before
Christmas. 2. Moore, Clement Clarke, 1779-1863—
Biography. 3. Poets, American—19th century—Biography. 4.
Chelsea (Manhattan, New York, N.Y.)—Biography. 5.
Christmas in literature. I. Del Re, Patricia, 1944- . II. Title.
PS2429.M5N533   1991
811'.2—dc20
[B]   91-11419

Grateful acknowledgment is made for permission to reproduce the following illustrations:

Pages 20, 22, 25, 37, 88: charcoal sketches by Susan Tammany. *Pages 27, 50, 57, 61:* I. N. Phelps Stokes Collection, Miriam & Ira D. Wallach Division of Art, Prints and Photographs, The New York Public Library, Astor, Lenox, and Tilden Foundations. *Page 75:* Eno Collection, Miriam & Ira D. Wallach Division of Art, Prints and Photographs, The New York Public Library, Astor, Lenox and Tilden Foundations. *Page 30:* Courtesy of the New York Historical Society, N.Y.C. *Page 65:* Museum of the City of New York. *Pages 84, 114:* Courtesy of General Theological Seminary.

Printed in the United States of America
Published by Pelican Publishing Company, Inc.
1000 Burmaster Street, Gretna, Louisiana 70053

This book is dedicated to
Charles and Marion Martin

Contents

Preface

 WAS the Night Before Christmas'' is the best-known poem in the English language. Children often learn the poem's first stanza before they learn their ABCs. The poem is the most published, re-published, illustrated, re-illustrated of all poems, with new offerings each Yuletide. '' 'Twas the Night Before Christmas'' is found in every medium of communication—television, film, radio, plays, recordings, computer, tapes, books, magazines, comic books, coloring books, pamphlets, newspapers, and puzzles—and on Christmas stamps, cards, and seals. The poem has been put to music; it is found in books of Braille. '' 'Twas the Night Before Christmas'' has been imitated, parodied, used in television commercials. The poem ranks in stature with such masterpieces as ''Silent Night'' and

Charles Dickens's *A Christmas Carol*. Passed on from one generation to the next, Christmas after Christmas, the poem's beauty, neatness, and ingenuity may be compared with the intricate mechanism of a clock or a music box. The poem has suspense, nostalgia, comedy, and most of all a sense of love and benevolence. It is a complete story, one with a beginning, a middle, and an end, that rivals many a great tale.

Even Clement Clarke Moore could not have envisioned " 'Twas the Night Before Christmas" riding across the centuries, a timeless poem forever brightening the hearts of boys and girls, men and women, everywhere.

Over the past forty years, due in large part to ever-expanding means of communication, films, television, computer, Clement Clarke Moore's " 'Twas the Night Before Christmas" has won millions of new friends. A curious public of lads and lasses and their parents, everywhere, have found delight in this world-renowned Christmas poem, yet little is really known of how it came to be. Even less is known of the man who wrote it.

When we think of a "Christmas" poem being included in anthologies of some of the world's greatest literature, anthologies listing classic works by Dryden, Tennyson, Shakespeare, Milton, Longfellow, and modern poets like

Robert Frost and Emily Dickinson, we can only marvel. It is perhaps the more remarkable because the poem was written by a man who believed at the time that he was composing a mere "children's" ballad.

What makes " 'Twas the Night Before Christmas," or "A Visit from St. Nicholas," unique among poems is the attention lavished on it, giving it, by some accounts, the most exposure ever accorded any poem ever written. This attention is not hard to understand when one realizes that no Christmas ever passes without publishers, large and small, issuing new editions of the poem, set against countless new illustrations. Scholar and perfectionist that he was, Moore produced a work of extraordinary literary merit, a poem with the power to hold the attention of even the most discriminating of readers—a work that children and adults seem never to outgrow.

Clement Clarke Moore created a work that stands alone as the most widely read and recited of poems. Millions of parents perform the happy ritual each year, sharing this warm and joyful anticipation of Christmas with their own little ones as their parents had when they were children. Moore could not have envisioned that he was writing a timeless classic, a masterpiece of such charisma, to become the most widely published poem ever. And now, a look at the life of this man and how " 'Twas the Night Before Christmas" came to be . . .

Acknowledgments

We would like to express our immense
gratitude to Patrick LoBrutto for
lending his editoral skills and
insights in behalf of this book.
Further gratitude is expressed to
Patricia Kossmann, who first saw it all.
And to Ralph Burger, Arthur Martinson,
Rev. Newton Willoughby, Patrick O'Hagen,
Bruce Parker, and Anne Racanelli
for their kindness and encouragement.

"There does not appear to have been another like the Christmas Eve when Margaret, Charity, Benjamin, Mary, Clement and Emily first heard their 'Dear father' introduce St. Nicholas at Chelsea house."

Charity Moore
The poet's mother

American Roots and Forebears

 WAS the Night Before Christmas'' was written by a man of wealth and lineage; among his antecedents Clement Clarke Moore could claim earls.

John Moor (without the *e*) was in 1609 the first of the poet's family to journey to the New World, entering New York Harbor on the vessel *Half Moon* with Henry Hudson. Though the Christmas poet's roots were essentially English, there were traces of Scottish, French, and Irish. May we assume his poetic bent was due to his Irish stock?

Some years later, a Reverend John Moore sailed from England to America. A clergyman of the Anglican faith, he was the poet's first direct ancestor in America. The Reverend Mr. Moore settled in Lynn, Massachusetts, where he became involved in helping to establish the New England colonies. In the middle of the seventeenth century, the Reverend Mr. Moore pulled up stakes, settling at the outset in Newtown, Long Island, now Elmhurst. Mr. Moore was an honest man, beloved by the Indians for his kindness and fair dealings in matters of trade. He was so admired by the Indians that they taught him the art of growing various kinds of apples. From his orchards came the Newtown Pippin, for which Moore became famous—and very wealthy as well.

Descended from the Reverend Mr. Moore was one Samuel Moore, who married Sarah Fish and had two sons. One of them, Benjamin Moore, was born November 5, 1748, at Newtown. Benjamin was tutored by his father, and at seventeen he entered Kings College (now Columbia University), graduating first in his class in 1768. After graduation, Benjamin Moore was taught theology privately by the rector of Trinity Episcopal Church in Manhattan, as preparation for the ministry. Journeying to England, he was ordained a deacon, then a priest in 1771. Upon his return to America, Moore was assigned to Trinity Church and its chapels. In 1775 his alma mater, Columbia, appointed him its president pro tempore.

Amid his busy life of religious and academic duties, Moore, at the age of thirty, found time to take a spouse. Listed among his flock was a widow, Mary Stillwell

Clarke. Mrs. Clarke had a daughter, Charity, age thirty-one, a spritely, lovely, and articulate young woman of aristocratic lineage. Charity and her mother were forever bickering over their loyalties to their countries. Charity favored the new nation, America, while her mother, who could count among her relatives lords and ladies, favored England.

The Clarkes lived at Chelsea House, a vast estate not far from what is today Greenwich Village. Paying the Clarkes a call was always a pleasurable experience for Benjamin Moore, since Mary Stillwell, known to her friends as Molly, was the perfect hostess. She entertained the hope of marrying off her daughter, but of course the suitor would have to be an aristocrat.

Charity, it seems, was most taken by the charming, kindly, and attentive Mr. Moore. They fell in love and on April 30, 1778, the Reverend Benjamin Moore and Charity Clarke were wed at Trinity Church.

On July 15, 1779, a son was born to them, their only child. On August 11 of that same year, the infant was christened Clement Clarke Moore.

Tribute to Chelsea

 HANDSOME Captain Thomas Clarke, grandfather of Clement Clarke Moore, was born in England on August 11, 1692. In the year 1745, at the age of fifty-three, Captain Clarke married the beautiful Mary Stillwell.

CAPTAIN THOMAS CLARKE

With the advent of the French and Indian War of 1754–1763, Captain Clarke was assigned to the New World to participate in the hostilities. The captain could not know that he was leaving his homeland forever. With him were his wife, Mary, and the eldest of their five children, a daughter named Charity.

Having survived the war, Captain Clarke made a decision to remain in the New World. It was a decision painfully shared by his spouse, for England was her heart and soul.

Crossing to America from Canada around 1765, Captain Clarke purchased ninety-four acres of prime New York land situated on a pleasant rise overlooking the Hudson River. The land was located on what is today called the West Side of Manhattan. It was bounded by Nineteenth to Twenty-fourth streets and from Eighth to Tenth avenues. The land was lush and proved most fruitful—virgin acres of marshes, meadows, trees, and rich farming soil. So pleased was the captain with his purchase that he named his estate Chelsea in tribute to the London hospital of the same name, which cared for wounded and aged British veterans. Clarke built his house, a strong wooden structure, and made it a comfortable home for his wife and daughter. He tamed the land into farms and gardens, and planted more trees—walnuts, oaks, maples, weeping willows, and sycamores. The winds from the Hudson River were soothing upon Chelsea in spring and summer, bitter and fierce by winter.

Their early years in the New World seemed to have been happy years, but darkness was to touch the lives of the Clarkes. The winds of revolution had begun to stir in the early 1770s. The American Revolution would pit American inhabitants still loyal to the king of England (George III) against Americans seeking independence.

It is perhaps his good fortune that Captain Clarke would not live to see the American Revolution, for his allegiance most certainly would have been torn between

MARY STILLWELL CLARKE

the land of his birth and the new land in which he had chosen to live out his life. On a bitterly freezing day in February 1774, the Clarkes' lovely Chelsea home burned to the ground. Charity and her mother were able to escape without injury, but the captain was not. Sustaining serious burns, he was taken some distance to a neighbor's farm. Captain Clarke lingered near death for two years before he expired peacefully in the arms of his wife. He did not live to see the marriage of his daughter Charity to Benjamin Moore, nor the birth of the grandson who bore his name as part of his own.

Mary Stillwell set about the task of rebuilding the Chelsea homestead, constructing a house of brick that would stand for over three quarters of a century and be inhabited by many happy grandchildren.

Mary's life would close just before the turn of the century.

3

The Poet's Early Years

LEMENT Clarke Moore was soundly educated as a child. He was tutored by Benjamin, his father, in French, Greek, Hebrew, and Latin, as well as in mathematics and science. Benjamin Moore also taught his son to love literature: Plato, Aristotle, Homer, and Virgil, and such famous Oriental works as the "Thousand and One Nights" of Omar Khayyám.

Eventually Clement Moore would study more difficult works of Oriental letters: the Sanskrit drama "Charudatta" by a fourth-century writer and "The Little Clay Cart," by Bhasa, the third-century writer; Japan's Kabuki dramatist Takeda Izumo's masterpiece, "Chushingura"; the father of Chinese drama, Kuan Hanch-'ing's "The Injustice Done to Maid Tou"; and "The Story of the Chalk Circle," by Li Ch'ien-fu. There were

CLEMENT CLARKE MOORE AS A BOY

also Bible studies, the Psalms, the New and Old Testaments. It always seemed there was little time for play, he would confide to his wise and attentive mother. ''Plenty of time for play,'' she would say, as the family dog raised his ears at the word *play*. ''One day, my son,'' she would continue, ''this''—looking about the vast Chelsea property, ''will be entrusted unto your stewardship. You will need wisdom and common sense if you are to manage it properly. You will have sons and daughters.'' Young Clement would wince at the thought of children, for he knew that entailed girls and marriage.

His mother and father also hired a music teacher, and the young lad learned the violin, while trips down to Trinity Church were an opportunity to learn the organ.

Like his father almost thirty years before, Moore graduated Columbia in his teens, in 1798. Again like his father, Clement Clarke Moore graduated highest in his class. In 1800 his father was appointed president of Columbia on a full-time basis. The following year, in an impressive ceremony, the Reverend Mr. Benjamin Moore was consecrated coadjutor bishop of New York, the same year his son took his master's degree at Columbia.

The early years of the new century found the young Moore enjoying a distinguished circle of friends, among them, mayor (and future governor) of New York De Witt Clinton, Francis Scott Key, Washington Irving, Alexan-

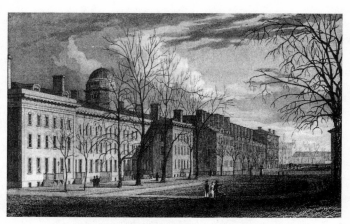

COLUMBIA COLLEGE, NEW YORK CITY, 1831

der Hamilton, Aaron Burr (a distant relative through marriage), and John Jay. Indeed, the fact that Clement's father was coadjutor bishop of the New York diocese brought the young man into immediate contact with famous civic, academic, and religious personages. All were often guests at the Chelsea homestead.

The start of the nineteenth century also brought rapid development to Manhattan. The island was becoming the business and financial center of the new nation. Clement Moore had already contemplated the possibility of its encroachment upon pastoral Chelsea. It was often the topic of conversation between his parents while the family dined. Young Moore had to be concerned, for he was by now well aware that with time he would become the patriarch of its ninety-four lovely acres. He watched and listened and learned from his mentor and close friend, his father. Their moments together had to be highly cherished, since Benjamin Moore's many religious and academic duties kept him away from home all too often.

But it happened that Bishop Moore was at Chelsea Homestead on July 11, 1804, when a horseman rode off Bloomingdale Road and up the lane that led to the house. Bishop Moore was told to come quickly to Greenwich Village, about a mile from Chelsea. The United States Secretary of the Treasury, Alexander Hamilton, had been seriously wounded in a gun duel with Vice President Aaron Burr. Bishop Moore, stunned, could only sigh, ''Such madness.'' Hamilton had been rowed across the Hudson from Weehawken, New Jersey, the site of the duel. Hamilton and Burr had been feuding ever since the secretary of the treasury had thrown his support to Thomas Jefferson instead of Burr in his bid for the presidency in 1800, forcing Burr to accept the second spot of vice president. All the Moores hoped that the messenger was mistaken in his assessment of Hamilton's condition as conveyed by the attending physician. Both Hamilton and Burr had been guests of the Moores many times; both men were handsome, charming, and affable—but ambitious as well. The Moores were very fond of both men. The fact that Hamilton's son Phillip had lost his life in a gun duel only two years before at the same Weehawken location must have been on their minds.

Bishop Moore was at first reluctant to accompany the messenger because of the religious prohibition against dueling, which made potential murderers out of both parties. Nevertheless, he was persuaded to accompany the horseman, calling for his coach and footman. Bishop Moore knew Hamilton to be a good man, the loving father of seven children. He had known him from his days as the temporary president of Columbia. Even then, President Moore had known of Hamilton's feisty ways; Hamilton had called for the previous college president to resign, which eventually paved the way for Moore's appointment.

Arriving at the home of a William Bayard on Jane Street in the village, Bishop Moore saw immediately that Hamilton's condition was grave. A bullet was lodged in his abdomen.

The dying man begged Moore to admit him to the Episcopal Church and give him the last rites. Only after the bishop was convinced of Hamilton's sorrow for having engaged in a life-threatening incident did Bishop Moore relent. Alexander Hamilton was given the last rites.

THE REVEREND BENJAMIN MOORE,
BISHOP OF NEW YORK, 1801

As the bishop's coach rounded Bloomingdale Road into Chelsea Lane, Charity and her son knew that their friend, one of America's most brilliant founding fathers, was gone.

4

Cupid on the Morrow

CHOLARLY pursuits continued to occupy young Moore's time after his days at Columbia. One project close to his heart for some time was the creation of a dictionary on the Hebrew language. From about 1804 Moore immersed himself in the lexicon. The work, titled *The Compendious Lexicon of the Hebrew Language* (in two volumes), was completed in 1809. It marked the first time that such a publication had been produced in America. The young man was proud of the work and found he enjoyed writing. In 1806, he contributed to a new translation with notes on the *Third Satire of Juvenal,* by a scholar named John Deur. Moore also wrote a treatise on various breeds of sheep. On the lighter side, the future Christmas poet dabbled in the creation of light verse; this seemed to bring him the greatest pleasure.

However, life was not all work for Moore. Always a close-knit family, the Moores enjoyed picnics, trips to the seashore, horseback riding, visits to the theater, and entertaining guests at dinner parties. At such times, music quartets were invited to perform for the guests, and Moore, being an amateur violinist, would participate. He was already an accomplished organist.

If his parents ever wondered when their son would choose a profession, no record of any such concern survives. In his early youth it was believed that he would prepare for the ministry. Both mother and father no doubt also wondered if their son would one day take a wife and settle down, for he was approaching his mid-thirties. They certainly could not have missed the occasional belles that stopped by Chelsea Homestead to inquire about their son, some leaving notes, others corresponding. Clement Clarke Moore was an eligible bachelor, highly refined, with a brilliant mind, a man of enormous wealth, a caring man, and handsome to boot. Little did they know that Cupid had already struck.

Even as the family was beginning to be concerned about the conflict between the United States and Great Britain known as the War of 1812, Clement was becoming enamored of a lovely young woman from New Jersey.

Soon, he would write private verses about Catherine Elizabeth Taylor:

Late from his guardian's favorite isle, . . .
A youthful, giddy, flirting maid,
Had come, he Cupid's plans to aid
With sparkling eye, with rosy cheek,
With tongue that loved full well to speak
In ev'ry way that best could tell
She was a laughing-loving belle.
Ah! who could dream this fluttering fair,
This outcast from Minerva's care
Could make her pupil heave a sigh,
And fill with love his thoughtful eye?
But, though it ne'er was dreamt nor thought,
Such was the wonder Cupid wrought.

Clement Clarke Moore had fallen in love.

His visits to Burlington, New Jersey, became more frequent. He wrote to his family of one of those visits:

> I yesterday wrote you a little bit of a letter, to let you know of my safe arrival here. I fear I shall not be able to write you one much longer today; I am sitting in Mrs. Taylor's parlour with Miss Taylor on the opposite side of the table. Of course, you may suppose my thoughts are not very firmly riveted to my paper. If I am not absolutely bewitched and rendered stone blind, I feel more & more assured that none of us will have reason to repent my rashness.

Soon, his beloved family would receive letters describing the courtship: "I pass [*almost the whole* crossed out] a great part of every day at Mrs. Taylor's, reading novels to her daughter, sometimes laughing & sometimes crying over them with her; we ramble about in the country and talk all manner of nonsense; I cut our names upon the trees and try, without success, to make verses."

By October 1813, Moore's mind was made up and his plea became serious. He wrote to his mother: "You may be sure I shall not leave this place (if I leave it without Mrs. Taylor & her daughter) before I have persuaded my little girl to fix the time when she will give me her hand."

5

Marriage and Farewell

 LEMENT Clarke Moore was thirty-four years old and Catherine Elizabeth Taylor was nineteen when they were married on November 20, 1813, at St. John's Episcopal Church on Varick Street, New York City. She was to become known to the poet as Eliza. Their

CLEMENT CLARKE MOORE IN 1810

courtship was one of mutual love—a love expressed to each other and shared in letters with Moore's mother, Charity. Though warmly accepting her daughter-in-law, giving away an only son was not easy on Charity. Nevertheless, she grew to genuinely love Eliza. After all, Eliza was her son's choice, a choice that made him shine with such happiness that she could hardly wish to taint it with jealousy.

The poet enjoyed the fact that while Eliza was quite beautiful, she also had a sweet innocence that often caused him to refer to her as his "little girl" and "possessed of every quality which my heart could desire." As for Elizabeth, she was totally enamored of her fiancé, and particularly charmed by the eloquent love letters her spouse-to-be had written her. She obviously enjoyed being tenderly courted and hoped she would be worthy of his hand in marriage. She once wrote to Charity Moore, "I scarcely dare hope to realize those expectations which the attachment he honors me with, has led him to form of me; yet under his guidance, anxious as I am to be all he wishes me, I trust my prayers for the ability of making him happy will not be unsuccessful."

It was a marriage made in heaven. The poet was a sharing man who extended his love to Elizabeth's widowed mother, her sister (who was suffering from mental illness), and her hardworking brother, a bank clerk.

Eliza, who was almost overly attentive to her husband, was very proud to have won such a wonderful man. She was quite aware that other young ladies of high society wooed the seemingly aloof male creature of such high intellect and gracious manners.

Her husband could not have been more

CATHERINE TAYLOR MOORE

protective of his young bride, catering to her every whim as Eliza presented him with one child after another: Margaret, born in 1815; Charity, 1816; Benjamin, 1818; Mary, 1819; Clement, Jr., 1820; and Emily, in 1822.

With motherhood upon her, Eliza was up to her duties; nursing the little ones and watching them develop brought her much happiness. She was delighted to be in a happy household, where the cries and laughter of little children were music to her ears. Grandma Charity was more than wonderful with the children and never meddlesome, though she was bearing the heavy cross of her husband's illness. In 1811, Bishop Moore had suffered a stroke that left him paralyzed; he needed constant care and watching. Charity's mother, Mary Stillwell Clarke, had been a widow the last twenty-five years of her life; Grandma Charity seemed headed for the same plight.

On a cold winter day—February 29, 1816—Benjamin Moore gave up his spirit after seventy-eight years of life. New York's Episcopal Bishop John Hobart said of him at his funeral: "Benjamin Moore rose to public confidence and respect, and to general esteem by the force of talents and worth."

Grandma Charity bravely wiped the tears from her eyes and turned her complete attention to Eliza, the grandchildren, and her son. This son of hers was always the apple of her eye, the great pride of her life. He had his father's eyes, prominent nose, and very handsome, dignified features, enhanced by long sideburns. As he matured, she noticed that in spite of some hardships— Hamilton's death, constant worry over the health of Eliza and the children, and now his father's passing—her son nevertheless kept the twinkle in his eyes—the same twinkle that would one day be found in the eyes of St. Nick.

Grandma Charity was convinced that her son had made the right choice in marrying the charming and amiable Eliza. With the ensuing years, Eliza seemed to grow more beautiful, for motherhood suited her. Her dark brown eyes sparkled above her delicate pale cheeks, while her lovely soft black hair swept across one side of her forehead.

Like her husband, Eliza could boast of a distinguished lineage. Her father, William Taylor, had by many accounts been the Lord Chief Justice of Jamaica. Her forebears on her mother's side numbered among the first Dutch settlers to come to the New World.

It took her husband a very long time to weather the passing of his father, a true mentor if ever a son had one. Clement Clarke Moore missed his father's unassuming manner and their happily shared experiences. He enjoyed listening to his father tell of having attended George Washington's inauguration in 1784, though at that time he gave his loyalties to the British crown. He was bound by the religious oath of the Anglican Church, but nevertheless held Mr. Washington in high regard. The poet often found himself studying his father's sermons, carefully penned on scrolls, sermons he published in 1824. From his father's writings, he could not help seeing how near and dear was his vocation of imparting knowledge.

Consulting with his mother and Eliza, Clement Clarke Moore decided to become a teacher in hopes of having a share in the development of young minds, continuing the work of the father whose fond memory he carried always.

6

A Family Together

AUTUMN, 1822. Clement Clarke Moore enjoyed walks down country lanes, particularly in spring, summer, and autumn. The pastoral blessings of Chelsea Homestead afforded Moore the opportunity to inspect his walnut, pear, and apple trees, his vegetable gardens, and his flower gardens. Occasionally one, and sometimes all of the children and their mother accompanied the poet. Moore never ceased to be moved by some aspect of nature. Sometimes it was the simple sway of a field of daisies, the grand parade of orange and yellow butterflies, or the chirping and singing of robins. Always there was the ever-assuring voice of his Eliza sweetly breathing in his thoughts, melodious upon his soul. It was therapeutic and very restful to be with his loved ones after a busy day of teaching. They were such good children, with impeccable manners, so very curious about such things as what gives flowers their colors and fragrances, what creates will-o'-the wisp, or is it really the sea you hear as you hold a sea shell to your ear? They were amazed when their father told them that they were not hearing the sea, but the blood rushing through the veins in their ears. It is fair to say that the Moore children's greatest joy was the time spent with Papa.

Their mother, gentle but firm, could barely manage the children during those afternoons when their father returned from downtown Trinity parish. When Moore began as a professor at the General Theological Seminary, space was leased for its students at that location until the construction of their institution was completed. The seminary was on Chelsea land donated by the poet. Moore taught Greek and Oriental literature at Trinity. After the new facility was completed, he had to travel only some ten yards from his property to his classroom. His days at the school were mostly taken up with lectures on Homer's *Odyssey,* Virgil's *Aeneid,* and Oriental literature involving Chinese, Japanese, and Sanskrit studies. Days spent examining the play *Peach Blossom Fan,* by Kung Shang-jen (1648–1718), concerning the decline of the Ming dynasty (1368–1644), must have been mighty heady stuff to the young men newly exposed to the world's great works.

For his children there were the tales of the *Arabian Nights* as told by Scheherazade. His children loved "Sinbad" and "Aladdin and His Magic Lamp," as told by their father in his own inimitable style. Eliza also shared their enthusiasm, for during their courtship, Moore had read her those same tales. His children were fascinated by the details of his days at the seminary: the number of students, when they rose in the morning (6:30), and their studies in Scripture, ecclesiastical history, pastoral theology—simply, they loved hearing about his work.

After these fulfilling days, he would enter his lovely home for a supper prepared by the servants. During the warmer months, the windows of Chelsea house were wide open, inviting in the warm summer breezes from the Hudson, saturated with the fragrance of clover. After grace, the family settled down to a hearty meal of barley soup, lamb or chicken or partridge, sweet potatoes, vegetables, and for dessert, apple pie, tea for Eliza, wine for the poet, milk for the children. While at the table, the children were never to speak unless addressed, though they could raise their hands if it was absolutely necessary that they be heard from. The poet was always quick to comment on the taste and preparation of the food, complimenting the servants if a dish was prepared to the family's liking.

On Sundays and holidays, the household staff broke bread with the Moores, and though they were servants, Moore treated them like family, attending to all their needs. They occupied a private suite of rooms on the fourth floor. At the table, tiny Emily was fed by Eliza, and there were always giggles from the other children if the littlest child spit out her food or threw her plate. Eliza would gently tap her little fingers, but when she cried, her mother always felt pangs of regret. Clement never interfered and rarely disciplined the children, believing what their mother said and did regarding the children was always correct and for their own good. After dinner, everyone would repair to the side porch for some cool lemonade and star gazing, particularly observing the Big Dipper and the North Star.

Moore found himself particularly concerned at the outset of 1822, for a yellow fever epidemic had begun. By the grace of God, Moore's family was spared the dreaded scourge that had afflicted so many in the developed part of Manhattan. Eliza had given birth to Emily only some months before, and nursing the child was sapping her strength. Soon, the hot summer waned as autumn breezes began chasing the torrid winds of August.

Eliza was an affectionate spouse, but in the presence of the children, the most she would do was take her husband's hand while their eyes traded the most tender messages of love. Occasionally, however, if her husband was overdue from the city, thus causing her anxiety, her heart would be so filled with rapture at his return that Eliza would throw herself into his consoling embrace. Without him, this woman, not really blessed with the tenacious heart of Grandma Charity, would have lost her spirit. While some of the woman servants could easily have assisted her in some of her motherly chores, Eliza jealously guarded every aspect of the children's rearing. Their father, of course, wanted his sons to attend Columbia, as he had and his father had. It was his hope that the girls would grow up and marry God-fearing, good men. It was his habit to put the children to bed with their mother at his side. Together they would listen to their night prayers.

At such times Moore relished passing on a bit of family history to the children. Their eyes widened when he told them how their great-grandmother was visited by General George Washington. On her complaint that the Continental soldiers billeted on her property during the early years of the Revolution had caused her untold distress—entering her new house, eating, and trampling upon her furniture—Washington promised that her trials at the hands of his army would end. The general was as good as his word; never again was she bothered by his soldiers. And though, until her death, she never wavered in her allegiance to her homeland, George Washington won great-grandma Stillwell Clarke's respect and admiration.

On the other hand, when the Hessian soldiers (German mercenaries in the British pay) were stationed on the Chelsea property, the widow Clarke was aghast to find them cutting down her precious trees for fires to keep themselves warm. This brave woman showed such rage that the Hessian soldiers let her trees be.

Moore also told them the story about his grandmother returning from the city one day to be stopped by a Continental soldier who told her a British cannonball had smashed into her house. Undaunted, she surveyed the damage. She never fixed the wall of her house, allowing the spot to remain for many years after.

Then there was Captain James Moore, a distant relative who was with George Washington on Christmas night in 1776 for the historic crossing of the Delaware. The captain lost his life that night in the service of his country.

When the children wanted to hear more of their brave forebears, Eliza would touch her husband's arm, for she was sleepy. The children would smile, give their mother and father a big hug, and say good-night. Eliza would draw open the curtains of their sleeping room, allowing the bright moon to shine in the window, and the children would soon fall asleep.

7

New York City in 1822

N 1822, Manhattan Island—12.5 miles long, 2.5 miles wide, with a total area of 22.6 square miles—was growing by leaps and bounds. It was already the political, financial, business, manufacturing, and seaport center of the young United States. The New York Stock Exchange had been fully established in the year 1817, the same year a host of banks won their charters to conduct business in New York City. By 1822, Wall Street was already internationally known. With the second Trinity Church (we today have the pleasure of its third incarnation) at its head, Wall Street was a street lined with stores and churches. Homes of the old Dutch were still visible throughout the area until the great fire of 1835 destroyed the last of them.

By this time New York had replaced Philadelphia as

VIEW OF WALL STREET, TRINITY CHURCH, AND THE PRESBYTERIAN
MEETING HOUSE IN 1825

the literary capital of the young nation. James Fenimore
Cooper, who dubbed New York ". . . a hobbledehoy
metropolis, a rag fair sort of place," moved to the city in
1822 to be closer to his publisher. Cooper, already famous, was about to reach the height of his career.
Lorenzo da Ponte was fresh from his triumphs as

Mozart's librettist for *Don Giovanni, Cosi fan Tutti,* and *Figaro* when he moved to New York at the urging of his friend Clement Clarke Moore. Da Ponte opened a bookshop and became professor of Italian at Columbia. A few years later, he would open the first Italian opera house in the United States, in Manhattan.

Yet there were farms on Broadway, and Yorkville, Greenwich, Bloomingdale, Harlem, and Chelsea were still virtually pristine. This "hobbledehoy metropolis" was a curious mixture of countrified and cosmopolitan.

In this year of 1822, a massive building boom was taking place, a boom extending northward from the Battery region of the city almost four miles uptown to about Fourteenth Street. By 1825, Greenwich Village would be absorbed into the urban fold of Manhattan. Moore's Chelsea would follow after.

The poet, an astute businessman, was well aware of this, for as early as 1811, the city planning commission had mapped out a plan for streets stretching to One Hundred Fifty-fifth Street. No United States city was growing faster. Already the eastside waterfront, with its mile of wharfs and warehouses, was host to hundreds of cargo vessels a month, ships importing myriad dry goods and perishables, textiles, tea, spices, and toys. Ships also brought immigrants. An equal number of vessels exported New World goods to Europe: cotton, wool, molasses, sugar, and flour.

The Manhattan waterfront was busy with agents and brokers who insured ships and cargos. Custom houses were established, and raked in enormous revenues. Waterfront labor loaded outgoing vessels with American goods and unloaded incoming ships, getting the goods to wholesalers and retailers who marketed them across the developing nation. Waterfront shipbuilding and manufacturing could barely keep up with the demands for goods, while a labor force from England, Scandinavia, the Netherlands, Germany, and Ireland beseiged the tiny island to find jobs. Added to this Babel in the ever-busier streets were the voices of fugitives from South America, Cuba, and Mexico—all of which were undergoing a series of bloody revolutions. New York drew strong men determined to survive and women with dreams of husbands, homes, and children.

The early Dutch settlers of the seventeenth century had passed the word along that Manhattan was the greatest place in the New World to win one's hopes and dreams if not afraid of endless toil. The west side of Manhattan, blessed with the Hudson River, fed Manhattan Island with legions of barges bringing in fur, wool, coal, Dutchess County beef and pork, livestock, and hundreds of horses from upstate and New Jersey communities. The Hudson would become even busier in 1825, when the Erie Canal—''Clinton's Ditch''— was completed. The barges would bring the riches of

the West and up-
state New York, for
New York City to
distribute to the
world. No river
was more abundant
in shad, and the
Hudson was also
the principal source
of ice for Manhat-
tan's businesses and
the community at
large.

Manhattan devel-
opers in 1822 were
fast buying up prop-
erty to meet the

DUTCH ARCHITECTURE—OLD HOUSE
IN BROAD STREET

growing population. Fur magnate John Astor was only
one of the many land barons who gobbled up property,
particularly waterfront land. In 1822, families such as the
Wendels, Goelets, and Rhinelanders were the big land
developers of Manhattan.

Machine politics was taking shape as Tammany Hall
was beginning to affect various facets of city govern-
ment. City Hall opened in 1812, and by 1822 its officials
would preside over a population of 160,000. The mayor

was James Allen; the governor, DeWitt Clinton; the United States president, James Monroe.

By 1822, children of New York were attending public school. The Free School Society, founded in 1805 under Mayor DeWitt Clinton, was serving some five thousand children, most of whom went to school for about three years. Children of the wealthy attended private schools, and most often young men went on to institutions of higher education—Columbia College in Manhattan, Yale, or Harvard—to prepare for the business world.

Medical care was available for all at several city hospitals, the most popular being Bellevue, whose history dated back to 1794. However, in 1822 many of the poor of Manhattan relied on quick fixes from home remedies and superstitions learned from the old country, or looked to the numerous quacks who sold bottles of patent medicine for a quarter and offered a "pill for every ill."

The city police force was made up of constables who kept order by day and watchmen who guarded the oil lamps that lit the streets by night. The watchmen of night also listed among their duties the act of crying the hours: "Twelve o'clock, a cloudy night. All's well." . . . "Two o'clock, the stars are shining. The moon is bright and full. All's well." Special rattles carried by such watchmen announced fires.

NEW YORK CITY, JUST BELOW CANAL STREET, 1800

These were the last days of a relatively crime-free New York. The old clapboard cottages and tenements built on fill in Collect Pond had begun to crumble or sink, and respectable people were moving to other neighborhoods. The intersection of Cross, Anthony, Little Water, Orange, and Mulberry streets, already known as the Five Points, would by the 1840s become the most dismal slum in America; Dickens was to compare it to the Seven Dials and Whitechapel districts of London. But in 1822, the Five Points—which for a century after would unleash gangsters like Danny Lyons and Danny Driscoll and Johnny Torrio and Al Capone—was mostly given over to beer drinking and dance halls.

Manhattan in 1822, despite the Hudson River, had a poor water system. New Yorkers could draw water from several sources, among them the Knapp Springs, special pumps, and the Manhattan water company, established in 1799 by Aaron Burr and his business associates. Some fortunates also had their own private wells. To avoid drinking the foul city water, those that could afford it purchased carbonated water or frequented the numerous saloons for beer or spirits.

The city fire department was on a voluntary basis, saddled with outmoded and inefficient equipment. Due to the poor water supply, blazes too often got out of control, with much life and property lost. Former mayor Philip Hone once remarked, ''Fires were so frequent in New York that visitors regarded them as one of the city's tourist sights.''

In winter, water outlets for putting out fires were often frozen solid. New fire codes did away with shingle-roofed houses built of wood, in favor of stone and brick houses with slanted roofs and chimneys that were to be cleaned and repaired regularly. For the most part, the Manhattan houses of 1822 subscribed to the Federal architectural style, which had prevailed since the Revolutionary War (1775–1783). Houses were two, three, and four stories of cheerful red brick or brownstone with stoops and iron railings in neat rows with simply ornamented facades. Interiors had high ceilings, large windows, mahogany furniture, marble tables and fireplaces.

The floor plans usually included dining rooms, front and back parlors, and upper floors for sleeping. Hallways on the upper floors concealed chamber pots and wash basins. There was a basement for the kitchen, and in some instances a vault room extended underneath the street in front of the house for food and firewood storage.

If you were poor in 1822 Manhattan, you lived under modest housing conditions: rents averaged from seventy-five cents to one dollar and twenty-five cents for a single room a week to six dollars for an apartment. Houses were heated with fireplaces fueled mostly with wood, but the poor were always cold. Their rooms, often cellar dwellings, were chilly, damp, and dirty. Lamps fueled by whale, fish, and vegetable oil and tallow candles provided illumination. The poor often slept in their street clothes and wore nightcaps to keep warm. Mice, even rats, might also be found in the dwellings of the poor, but were tolerated, for most people were grateful to have any kind of roof over their heads. If a tenant was dissatisfied with his room or apartment, a complaint to the landlord could well result in eviction. A vacancy sign was immediately put out, and the rooms would quickly be filled by another hapless tenant. There was no city agency to complain to.

The tenant of the typical city dwelling of 1822 washed from street-pump water, though one could take a free bath at one of the bathhouses provided for Manhattan residents by generous philanthropists. There were no such luxuries as bathtubs or showers. Clothes were washed in the rivers, by the backyard well, or with street-pump water. Toilets or wooden privies were located in backyards. Manhattan's sewer system had not been established by 1822; that would not be realized until about 1850. These conditions, coupled with crowded tenements, provided ideal breeding grounds for such scourges as smallpox, yellow fever, measles, mumps, and cholera.

The city streets of 1822 Manhattan were of cobblestone and uneven pavement, wooden planks, or just plain dirt. They were filthy and inhabited not only by the mass of pedestrians, but by household pigs that roamed freely to scavenge from garbage strewn everywhere. In summer, when the mercury might climb into the upper nineties, the stench was noxious; flies, rats, and mice were as ubiquitous as the children playing in the filth.

In 1822, a severe outbreak of yellow fever hit the city. Many people died, but many escaped to the surburb of Greenwich Village. Among the throngs that found refuge from the disease were many businessmen and professionals who remained in the village to resume their businesses and practice their trades. Before long, Greenwich

Village was no longer countrified, as buildings went up to meet the demand for apartment dwellings and business establishments.

Conveyance in 1822 in Manhattan and beyond was by carriage and coach drawn by any number of horses. In winter, when the snow could accumulate in feet, runners were fitted to the carriages. Carriage houses and stables with hay, feed, and blacksmiths took care of the animals and carriages the way auto shops care for cars today.

Manhattan streets of 1822 were lively with vendors who hawked: "Gingerbread hot from the oven!" "Oysters to melt in your mouth!" "Chestnuts! Don't burn your fingers!" "Fresh violets for your sweetheart!" For three cents, one could buy roast pigeon from a street vendor. One pathetic sight was poor little girls hawking bunches of radishes, purchased by passersby not so much out of need as out of sympathy, for few liked the taste of radishes. Meat wagons, butcher shops on wheels, delivered city-inspected meat to favorite customers. Much of the meat was preserved with salt. In summer, ice wagons could hardly keep up with the demand for ice to preserve perishables and chill lemonade.

Manhattan in 1822 was surrounded by farms that grew a multitude of vegetables; the potato was considered by some to be as deadly as toxic nightshade. Other vegetables were also suspect, notably the tomato. Dairy

BROADWAY FROM THE BOWLING GREEN, 1826

farms and orchards also served Manhattan. However, for the luxury of shopping, there was Broadway, a wide thoroughfare on the west side almost three miles long, and on the east side, the Bowery, one day to gain an unwholesome reputation. These two shopping districts were the toast of early Manhattan, where commodities such as dried beans, tea from China, coffee, brown sugar, flour, milk, churned butter, bread, salt, spices, and molasses were available. One could purchase chickens from the butcher for about six cents a pound, as well as turkeys, lamb, mutton, beef, ham, venison, rabbit, pheasants, and duck. Other shops sold household items such as curtains and carpets from Belgium and Persia; ladies' things, such as hosiery and gloves; jewelry, such as pretty pendants and gold earrings, fans, smelling salts, looking glasses, brushes, combs, handkerchiefs, fine linen corsets, beautiful ribbons from Paris, and perfume. For gentlemen there were handsome snuff boxes, razors, and hand warmers. Dress shops sold lovely bonnets of straw and made-to-order gowns and hoods.

In 1822, food was cooked in open fireplaces, meat often on a spit that was hand turned. Saloons served food as well as beer, wine, and whiskey.

The city building owner of 1822 could have his sidewalk cleaned or his wrought-iron gates polished by little boys who went about ringing doorbells. In this year of the birth of the immortal Christmas poem, a wealthy gentleman such as Clement Clarke Moore wore suits of fine broadcloth, felt or silk vests, often brightly colored and trimmed with brass buttons. A small vest pocket served to house a hand-wound pocket watch and its key. White shirts with ruffles and pleats were also the norm among the wealthy gentlemen of old New York. Often high hats were part of one's wardrobe. Pipes and snuff were widely used by men, and beards, whiskers, and mustaches enhanced a masculine appearance, seemingly preferred by the fairer sex of early America.

Ladies young and old wore flounced gowns, silk stockings, veils, delicate lace things, imported bonnets, feathered hats arrayed with colorful ribbons, and brocade slippers indoors. Outdoors, parasols were desired in summer, parasols that rivaled the colors of the rainbow, and, to fend off an autumn breeze, shawls of camel hair.

In 1822, women wore scant makeup, but orris root powder was widely used for a healthy yet delicate countenance. Much like today, a slender appearance, notably a tiny waist, was desired by stylish ladies who forced themselves into constricting corsets to achieve hourglass figures at the expense of their health. Those who were unable to afford the finer wardrobes of the rich wore homespun petticoats, bonnets, and footwear of calfskin for walking the city's dirt and mud side streets. Men wore checkered shirts, breeches, flannel and slouch hats cocked at the corners.

By 1822, a half-dozen newspapers existed, the most prevalent being the *New York Evening Post,* founded by Alexander Hamilton, and later to become the *New York Post.* Such newspapers were purchased by subscription and carried ads informing New Yorkers about the latest ribbons and fabrics from Paris, news stories about visiting dignitaries, items on crime, international events, the exploits of such tycoons as John Jacob Astor, and visits by a traveling animal show.

Two years before 1822, the city's first libraries were

established: the Mercantile Library and the Association of Apprentices Library. Such libraries made books available on a circulation basis and were used by citizens of moderate income.

November 1822 marked the opening of the 2,000-seat Park Theatre, an elegant structure to host opera, drama, and symphony music. Castle Clinton, a fort built just off the tip of Battery Park during the War of 1812, was two years from being converted into the famed Castle Garden. Theaters in those days were without numbered seats; the wealthy sent their servants to stand in line for choice locations. With the great Irish population in New York City, St. Patrick's Cathedral, built in 1815 on Prince Street, answered the spiritual needs of Manhattan's fastest growing group of immigrants. These newcomers found jobs as lamplighters, meat inspectors, constables (*C*onstables *O*n *P*atrol gave way to the acronym *COP*) and the future policemen of New York City.

Besides being the hotbed of commercial activity, the eastside waterfront was also the supplier of nightlife for thousands of seamen. Some two thousand saloons catered to the liquid needs of the seamen, while brothels existed to satisfy the promiscuous. Drinking and wild and lewd conduct were quietly tolerated by the powers that be, if for no other reason than that the money spent in the saloons helped fill the city coffers. Saloon crime

SOUTH STREET FROM MAIDEN LANE, 1828

was also a factor, with drinking brawls resulting in death and injury. Children were forbidden to be out after dark, while homeless children were placed in the local orphan asylum. The homeless adult could find warmth, food, and care at city alms houses. Public assistance was often available to out-of-work city dwellers, particularly to heads of families.

In 1822, Washington Square (in Greenwich Village), was a vast cemetery, the city's potter's field. Fifth Avenue would not be a street of note until much later in the century, and, in 1822, ran only as far as Thirteenth Street. Manhattan had no parks or children's playgrounds. A walk to Greenwich Village and beyond was a pastoral adventure. City children played in the streets or in back lots; hide-and-seek, tag, and some form of hopscotch were popular.

Wealthy Manhattanites attended balls, the theater, and private social clubs for entertainment, or chamber concerts and pianoforte recitals at the home of some high-society figure for an evening of Mozart, Scarlatti, or Corelli.

8

Winter and Christmas in Manhattan of 1822

ANHATTAN'S winter of 1822 was severely cold, as icy winds from the Hudson and East rivers whipped across the growing metropolis with gale force, often sending temperatures plunging below zero. Snow was the rule, lots of it, with the wind creating huge, hampering drifts. Horses left exposed to the wintry elements often froze to death.

Inside peoples' homes, roaring fires crackled in fireplaces constantly fed with logs. Children made extra pennies shoveling sidewalks and stoops, while streets, even main thoroughfares such as Broadway and the Bowery, remained snow laden. The city had not yet established its sanitation system; most certainly, snow-removal brigades were the farthest thing from its mind. Children, as they do today, loved the snow and the pleasant pastimes of snowball fights, building snowmen and snow castles, skating, and sled riding. These were some of the few blessings of the harsh winters. In 1822 there was no immunization for flu, and children and the aged often succumbed to the resulting pneumonia.

The familiar sight of food vendors prevailed at this season; hearty folks undaunted by cold and snow, they sold hot foods such as gingerbread, sweet toasted bread, and tea.

In 1822 New York, Christmas was a religious holiday. Generally, only children received presents. These were placed in hanging stockings, a holdover from the city's strong Dutch influence. Yule logs were burned, an English influence, and wreaths, a German influence, were found everywhere, as was holly and mistletoe. Lighted candles glowed in windows, and bonfires burned in the streets with little regard for the dangers of fires. The religious significance of the day was seen everywhere. Bells pealed, churches were crowded, and charity to the poor was prevalent; food and clothing were dispensed at the city's alms houses. Taverns were closed.

Children and grown-up carolers stood at designated spots singing Christmas carols, and the public stopped to listen, for there was not a lot of entertainment for the general public. Ice skating was a favorite form of recreation, and what better place for that than the solidly frozen Hudson River? Ice skates were popular Christmas gifts, as were hats, scarves, earmuffs, and mittens.

SNOW SCENE, CORNER OF WARREN AND GREENWICH STREETS, 1809

Sleigh riding was another Christmas pastime. City folks piled into a sleigh for a "frolic" or party, riding about Manhattan, sightseeing, visiting friends and family, jingling the bells, and singing. James Pierpoint was to immortalize the pastime with his classic "Jingle Bells" almost thirty-five years later, in 1856.

Christmas called for an oversized dinner with menus consisting of roast suckling pig, beef stew, turkey, ham, soups, Christmas pies, cookies, cider, eggnog, wassail, tea and coffee, and all manner of confections—sugar almonds, peppermints, chocolates, rock candy, and licorice.

There was singing and good cheer everywhere. Christmas in old New York was indeed a happy time.

9

First Flashes of a Christmas Masterpiece

HE Christmas recess was upon the Chelsea household. The Moore children, their mother, the servants, and the poet were looking forward to the most joyous holiday of the year. Some dolls had arrived at the household, ordered sometime before from Europe; from Grandma Charity's sisters in England came tightly packed cans of English plum pudding.

Moore was on his way into busy Manhattan, for the poet wished to purchase gifts in some of the shops. He had just paid a call to City Hall—about two miles from his Chelsea estate—to wish Mayor Stephen Allen a happy Christmas. Then it was off to Trinity churchyard to pray at the graves of his father and Alexander Hamilton, who was buried not far from the bishop.

Christmas was in the air, for even as he prayed, a children's choir somewhere in the vicinity could be heard singing the Christmas carols of old. The poet had been to his father's grave the week before with his mother. It was his habit to have her taken to the churchyard whenever she wished, though the harsh winter weather was a hindrance to her cherished visits. The carols on his mind, the poet smiled as he remembered how his father had loved to celebrate Christmas. Moore was thinking of how his father carefully supervised the Nativity scene at Trinity, seeing that every detail was perfect for the baby Jesus.

Finishing his prayers, Moore visited the rector of Trinity Church, where he saw the new statue of the Christ Child from Italy. The poet would attend Christmas Day services at his parish, St. Mark's Church, with his entire family, servants and all. After visiting Trinity Church, Moore was driven by his coachman, Patrick, to the Bowery. There he purchased some yarn, a set of silk and muslin curtains, some sugarplums imported from Germany, some goose-feather pens and India ink, and a silver teapot. He also purchased a case of French wine, some snuff, and a set of candles. At one store, the poet placed an order for a Belgian carpet and a large mirror. The poet closed out the shopping chores that he delighted in performing by purchasing expensive white bread, white sugar, and several pounds of coffee beans from Brazil. As a treat for old Patrick, he had his tobacco pouch filled with rich Raleigh, Carolina, tobacco.

As the poet was being driven back to Chelsea, he

suddenly ordered his coach stopped. This happened several times, for Moore liked to observe the large amount of building taking place. Just four years before, Moore privately published a pamphlet, ''Plain Statement Addressed to the Proprietors of Real Estate in the City County of New York, by a Landholder,'' a work in which the poet lashed out at the vast amount of indiscriminate development taking place in Manhattan. In spite of having many influential friends, among them Francis Scott Key, whose ''Defense of Fort Henry'' was to become known as ''The Star Spangled Banner''; Samuel B. Morse, of Morse Code fame; future mayor and millionaire Philip Horne; and John Henry Hobart, Episcopal bishop of New York, none could help him stem the tide of development that he knew would eventually overwhelm Chelsea. A city commission had already mapped out a plan for northward development of Manhattan that would cut across Chelsea. Moore could not realize how important his gift of land to the General Theological Seminary, to be completed in 1827, would become. Within thirty-five years after writing '' 'Twas the Night Before Christmas,'' the seminary on West Twenty-first Street would be all that was left of *his* Chelsea.

Moving along Broadway, through Greenwich Village, Moore ordered Patrick to stop the coach. The poet stepped out of the carriage. ''My, my,'' he mumbled to himself. It seemed that new red brick and brownstone

THE GREAT FIRE—1835 (CITY HALL AND PARK ROW)

structures had sprung up in just one week's time; with
them came a multitude of chimneys with their white and
black smoke dotting the twilight blue. The yellow fever
epidemic had caused a greater spurt of building than he
had anticipated. Moore was in his forties, and his sideburns were graying as he lifted his tophat to cool off, for
he was quite upset by what he viewed as a building spree.
Standing near the coach, Moore seemed preoccupied with
his thoughts for some time, and perhaps only the impa-
tient pair of white horses stamping and whinnying jolted
the poet from his thoughts.

The poet suddenly seemed like a new man, as if reju-
venated with new energy. Smiling to his coachman, he

chuckled, "Let's get on." The poet had managed to secure some special books through the New York Historical Society, of which he was a member, on the patron saint of children, St. Nicholas, much admired not only by children, but by him! Moore looked forward to spending some time in his private library, after the children were put to bed, for the study of St. Nicholas. He would like to have consulted with his close friend Washington Irving, but Irving had been in England since 1815. Irving had some unique ideas about St. Nicholas, and the more the poet thought about those ideas, as expressed in Irving's *Knickerbocker's History of New York,* the more he chuckled.

When the coach halted at the gates of Chelsea Homestead, Moore was laughing so hard, he barely noticed Patrick's extended hand waiting to assist him from the vehicle. Old Patrick pretended to be oblivious to what he must have viewed as giddiness. Moore at last said, "Oh, Patrick, my good man, I am thinking of St. Nick . . . a little old driver, so lively and quick. Yes, Patrick, I am overwhelmed with ideas." The poet was still laughing, but managed a few last words before hurrying indoors to his waiting family. Patrick chuckled, too, when he heard what sounded like a rhyme. To his surprise, he began to laugh as he found himself repeating what the poet had said: "He had a broad face, and a little round belly, that shook, when he laughed, like a bowl full of jelly."

10

Genesis of the Christmas Masterpiece

HE development of "A Visit from St. Nicholas" began in 1809, when Washington Irving, considered one of the greatest storytellers ever to have lived, wrote a satire on the early Dutch settlers of New Amsterdam. Irving titled his book *A History of New York from the Beginning of the World to the End of the Dynasty,* listing a fictitious Diedrich Knickerbocker as the author. The book was eventually to become known by the title *Knickerbocker's History of New York.* Within weeks of publication, it became a runaway bestseller. The public also learned that the true author of the work was not Diedrich Knickerbocker, but Washington Irving, native New Yorker. This was the same fellow who in 1801 and 1803 had poked gentle fun at the early Dutch settlers with a series of letters published in the *Morning Chronicle* and signed with the pen name Jonathon Old-style. That first edition of *Knickerbocker's History* struck up a storm of controversy, and Irving launched a powerful salvo at the Burghers (citizens of the town) by adding interesting facts about St. Nicholas, the protector of New Amsterdam (renamed New York after 1664).

What Irving wrote in *Knickerbocker's History* was to begin a series of changes in the European St. Nicholas of Myra brought to the New World. This was to have a profound effect on a poet friend of Irving's—Clement Clarke Moore, and that was to mean a profound, and permanent, alteration of the way St. Nick was to be perceived throughout the world.

In *Knickerbocker's History of New York,* through a character named Olaffe Van Kortlandt, Irving wrote:

> And the sage Olaffe dreamed a dream—and lo, the good St. Nicholas came riding over the tops of trees in that self-same wagon wherein he brings his yearly presents to children, and St. Nicholas sat beside Olaffe under the tree where he rested. He knew him by his broad hat and his long pipe and by the resemblance he bore to the figure on the bow of the *Goede Vrouw*.

The vessel that the first Dutch settlers sailed on in 1621 when they came to America was called the *Goede Vrouw* (Good Housewife).

St. Nicholas lit his pipe and the smoke from his pipe ascended into the air and spread like a cloud overhead. It spread over the countryside and Olaffe dreamed he climbed a tree and saw through the haze a vision of a great city with domes and spires. And when St. Nicholas had smoked his pipe, he twisted it in his hatband, and laying a finger beside his nose, gave the astonished Olaffe Van Kortlandt a very significant look; then remounting his wagon, he returned over the treetops and disappeared.

Irving also wrote:

At this early period was instituted that pious ceremony, still religiously observed in all our ancient families of the right breed, of hanging up a stocking in the chimney on St. Nicholas Eve, which is always found in the morning to be miraculously filled for good St. Nicholas has ever been a great gift-giver to children.

What had Washington Irving wrought? Like a painter never to know the value of a canvas in this lifetime, Irving would never realize the fruits of his book regarding St. Nicholas and Christmas. Only in the twentieth century would scholars discover the connection between Irving's satire on the early Dutch settlers of New York and Moore's " 'Twas the Night Before Christmas.''

Consider these comparisons:

> *Irving:* . . . and when St. Nicholas had smoked his pipe, the smoke from his pipe ascended into the air and spread like a cloud overhead.
>
> *Moore:* And the smoke it encircled his head like a wreath.
>
> *Irving:* And laying a finger beside his nose . . .
>
> *Moore:* And laying his finger aside of his nose . . .
>
> *Irving:* [St. Nicholas] gave Olaffe Van Kortlandt a very significant look; then remounting his wagon he returned over the treetops and disappeared.
>
> *Moore:* And giving a nod, up the chimney he rose.
>
> *Irving:* Which stocking is always found to be miraculously filled.
>
> *Moore:* He spoke not a word, but went straight to his work, and filled all the stockings . . .

The wagon ridden by St. Nicholas became a sleigh. While Irving's setting was the eve of St. Nicholas Day (December 6), Moore placed the time on the night before Christmas, or Christmas Eve.

But where did Moore find his idea for the sleigh and reindeer? In 1821, a book was published in New York for twenty-five cents a copy: *A New Year's Present to the Little Ones from Five to Twelve*. No author was listed.

WASHINGTON IRVING'S RESIDENCE ON THE HUDSON

Among eight colored engravings in the little book is one that depicts Santa in a sleigh being pulled by a single reindeer. This book was the first to connect reindeer with St. Nicholas. It was also the first book of its kind printed in America to use a Dutch derivative for St. Nicholas, "Santeclaus," as the bearer of gifts to children. Underneath the picture is found the poem:

> Old Santeclaus with much delight
> His reindeer drives this Frosty night.
> O'er chimney tops, and tracks of snow,
> To bring his yearly gifts.

11

St. Nicholas

 LEMENT Clarke Moore was not a frivolous man, and he was not about to profane St. Nicholas, or any saint, for that matter. Since Moore really knew little about St. Nicholas of Myra—the gift giver beloved by millions in Europe—he decided to consult some manuscripts to see if it was possible for St. Nicholas and he to journey into modern times.

Through careful study, he learned that in the fourth century St. Nicholas had saved three young girls from a life on the streets in the city of his birth—Patara, a seaport in the province of Lycia in Asia Minor. In that city there lived a man with three marriageable daughters who had fallen upon hard times. Since the distressed father could not afford dowries for each girl, they would surely not find husbands. With no recourse, the man resolved to sell his daughters into slavery or subject them to a life of ill-repute, lest his wife and younger children starve. It was an awful decision for a father, or anyone, to make, but the father tempered his dark plan with a prayer that God would forgive him his terrible deed. St. Nicholas learned of the man and his plight and, being from a wealthy family, the saint resolved to help the man anonymously. By night, under a moonless sky, the saint stole up to the father's abode, and finding an open window, left three bags of gold on the windowsill with instructions for how the money was to be used. The saint's instructions were heeded by the father, and the three daughters, each with a dowry, found a husband. The father repented and, discovering the name of his generous benefactor, told all who would listen of the wonder of St. Nicholas.

But it was the fact that St. Nicholas was the patron saint of children that most intrigued Moore. How did this come about? Clement Clarke Moore learned of the story of Basilios, one of the great legends that connect children and St. Nicholas. The story of Basilios began, after the death of the saint, on the eve of December 6, at Myra, where the saint had served as Bishop Nicholas. The people of Myra were celebrating his memory when pirates from Crete fell upon the city. A great deal of booty was seized, and a young boy named Basilios was carried off into slavery. The child was chosen by the emir of Crete to be his personal cupbearer, and served in that position for a year. On the following eve of St. Nicholas day, young Basilios' parents were in no mood to celebrate with the rest of the town, but as they were devout people, they made a quiet celebration at home. Suddenly the dogs of the house began to bark, causing the parents to rush out to the courtyard.

Had the terrible pirates returned? Consider their surprise and amazement when there were no pirates, but their little boy, wearing Arab clothes and carrying a goblet filled with wine. As in all miracles, the child's parents were filled with both terror and joy in that first moment. Their son Basilios explained that he was about to serve his master a cup of wine when a power had lifted him up and carried him off. He had been filled with fear, when St. Nicholas appeared to him, calmed him, and brought him home. St. Nicholas day had once again become a cause for rejoicing.

The poet smiled. Moore thought of his children: Margaret, Charity, Benjamin, Mary, Clement, Jr., Emily. Since he had always taught the children that St. Nicholas brought gifts on Christmas Eve, the setting of his poem would be Christmas Eve. Moore fiddled with his goose-quill pen before rising from his comfortable mahogany wingback chair. He went to the window. Pondering, Moore was momentarily struck by the bright moon shining upon a freshly fallen snow. Returning to his desk, he quickly dipped his quill in a small bottle of India ink and wrote: ''The moon on the breast of the new fallen snow, gave a lustre of mid-day to objects below.'' The tiny faces of his children again came to his mind: little Emily, cooing; Margaret, seemingly mature, though she was only seven; Charity, the child who once requested something from his quill for Christmas; the boys; the girls; his beautiful Eliza. How they could melt his heart!

Again he looked over his notes on St. Nicholas: The saint's mother's name was Nonna. Nonna had been barren until her conception of the future miracle worker, Nicholas. As a child, Nicholas had already devoted himself to the service of God.

Moore placed his pen aside. He thought of his children, fast asleep. He looked over another pair of lines of poetry he had written: ''The children were nestled all snug in their beds, while visions of sugarplums danced in their heads.''

The poem, he had to admit, was a delightful task, like nothing he had ever written. Nevertheless, the poet felt he had a reputation to uphold as a scholar and professor and respected businessman. He and Eliza had discussed his project, and he was quite pleasantly surprised when she sanctioned the idea. Both had decided that the poem would be for the children and remain in the family to be enjoyed each Christmas—if the children liked it. As for profaning St. Nicholas, the more he thought of how people accepted Washington Irving's ideas about St. Nicholas, the more the poet believed his version was feasible. Grandma Charity was also a model of encouragement. ''It is a pleasing idea,'' she said.

The poet had decided not to use the Dutch spelling of Santa Claus, because the children were more familiar with St. Nicholas. Meter was a factor pressing on his mind. Moore had always fancied himself a poet who could adhere to the discipline of the art form. He was grateful to Eliza for suggesting he save a poem he had seen in the *Spectator* on Christmas, 1815. Having spent the better part of the afternoon searching for the poem, he found it carefully tucked away in a drawer of his oak desk. ''Perfect meter,'' whispered Moore, as he read the poem:

> Oh good holy man!
> Whom we Sancte Claus name,
> The Nursery your praise
> Shall proclaim;
> The day of your joyful
> Visit returns,
> When each little bosom
> With gratitude burns,
> For the gifts which at night

You so kindly impart
For the girls of your love,
And the boys of your heart.
Oh! Come with your paniers
And pockets well stow'd,
Our stockings shall help you
To lighten your load,
And close to the fireside
Gaily they swing
While delighted we dream
Of the presents you bring.

Oh! Bring the bright Orange
So juicy and sweet,
Bring almonds and raisins
To heighten the treat:
Rich waffles and doughnuts
Must not be forgot,
Nor Crullers and Oley-Cooks
Fresh from the pot.
But of all these fine presents
Your Saintship can find,
Oh! Leave not the famous
Big Cookies behind—
Or, if in your hurry,
One thing you mislay,
Let that be the Rod—
And oh! keep it away.

Then holy St. Nicholas!
All the year,
Our books we will love
And our parents revere;
From naughty behavior
We'll always refrain,
In hopes that you'll come
And reward us again.

The poet of Christmas Eve returned to his work, scribbling happily until the wee hours.

12

Christmas Prelude to Immortality

HE Moores' Chelsea mansion was imposing against the wintry sky of Christmas Eve, 1822. Its four-story brick facade and low basement were dressed in white by a heavy snowfall. Elevated on a bluff, Chelsea House was exposed on all sides to the elements. The charming abode had three chimneys and many large windows. Its stately entrances in front and on one side of the structure were the gateways to the well-known Moore hospitality. It had been the home of the poet for many years—forty-three, to be exact—for the poet had been born at Chelsea Homestead, the house built by his grandmother, Mary Stillwell Clarke, almost fifty years before. She had ordered it built almost entirely of brick, for she vowed never to reside again in a house built of wood—fearing fire, which had taken her hus-

CHELSEA HOUSE, 1822

band, Thomas. The poet had added another floor to the house some years back, and all were proud to call Chelsea home.

Here was the threshold over which he had carried his bride with true, enduring love on that memorable day of their wedding. With winter upon Chelsea, the rolling hills—so beautiful with elms and chestnuts in spring, summer, and autumn—were bare. The wind whistled its wintry songs, never intruded upon by the bustling metropolis of Manhattan, less than a mile away.

The curtained windows of the living room emitted a faint glow as the hearth within burned brightly, offering warmth and heat for the evening dinner kettles and pots that hung above the fireplace flames. Lighted candle chandeliers and ornate lamps flickered softly, shedding generous light upon the beige walls decorated with watercolors of flowers and family portraits. A pair of huge bookcases held such classics as St. Thomas More's *Utopia,* volumes on ancient Rome such as *The Twelve Caesars* by Suetonius, Aristotle, Plato, and Homer, as well as a few works on etiquette of the day, copies of the poet's Hebrew lexicon, and others. The ceilings of the cozy house were high, and by day, the rooms—particularly the main parlor—were light and airy. In winter the curtains were most often drawn for maximum warmth, for with tiny children, colds were always a distinct possibility. The parlor floors were lined with thick green carpet, while large mirrors enhanced each parlor's brightness, rendering an air of gaiety. Everywhere there were mahogany wingback chairs and sturdy walnut and oak tables.

The most congenial and emotionally binding spot in the entire house lay within the immediate vicinity of the hearth in the main parlor. Here the poet told the children their favorite stories, and it was at the hearth that they shared their dreams of one day growing up, their joys, their sorrows. It was also at the hearth that the poet and his Eliza would often while away the evening hours after the children were put to bed, discussing the future, the past, the poet's concerns about the General Theological Seminary, and concerns about the children. They discussed the servants and a host of other matters ranging from the developing city of Manhattan to President Monroe's warnings to European powers against extending their systems to any part of the Western Hemisphere—to be presented officially the following year as The Monroe Doctrine.

Now it was Christmas Eve, and the children would soon have to be put to bed, but Clement Moore had not come home. The poet had left Eliza in the early afternoon, not staying for tea. He wished to go on several errands, first looking in on the construction of the General Theological Seminary on his property, then off with the coachman, Patrick, to purchase the largest turkey they could find. The pair had gone to the Washington Market at the tip of Manhattan, where the bird of their choice would be chosen from the thousands of turkeys gobbling in crowded pens, to be slaughtered for the Christmas feast.

The Seth Thomas clock chimed its Cambridge quarters, and as the last note tolled six, the sweet motif of sleigh bells streamed forth, heralding the arrival of the master of the house. The children chirped "Papa! Papa!" Just before her husband touched the brass knocker, Eliza sprang open the door, quite oblivious to the stream of frosty air and snow that blew inside. Dressed in a favorite gown, wearing a fragrant rose perfume, her hair thrown up in a bouffant coif, she looked ravishing as she fell into Moore's arms. Right behind the poet entered Patrick, his arms burdened with a large basket that contained food and a grand turkey. While a servant took the poet's top hat, other servants received the basket of goods from Patrick, for it would be their duty to prepare the Christmas feast. One by one, the children kissed their father's round, rosy, cold cheeks. Happiness arrested the poet's soul, and after being relieved of his heavy topcoat and large woolen mittens, a twinkle came to his eyes—such a twinkle as all had never seen before.

Eliza, the children, and the servants were filled with great anticipation. Eliza's eyes welled with tears, for she knew the little war raging within her husband's soul for the past weeks was over. Never in all their years together had her husband had such a burning desire to accomplish a task. She knew his poem had been completed; it was a personal triumph. He did not share the title of his new creation with her, nor with anyone, for that matter, but sometime during the day the poet had finished the little poem that would be his gift to his family. No one realized that it would bring him immortality.

The poet's eyes found Grandma Charity, and her expression told Clement to wait. Let all enjoy their dinner, then, as a reward, he might impart his Christmas poem to them. The poet, famished, found he was agreeable, and all sat down to a sumptuous meal. This night the children would not have to retire to their beds until Papa had bestowed upon them his Christmas treat.

CHARITY CLARKE MOORE

In the glow of the crackling fireplace, the children sat on the carpet at their father's feet while the servants and Grandma Charity relaxed in chairs. Eliza, holding Emily in her arms, stood afar, so happy for her husband. The poet gazed upon each of his children's happy little faces, bright with anticipation. Moore observed his servants, and they knew he loved them like part of the family. The poet saw the wise face of his mother, Grandma Charity. She had never looked more regal as she raised her head to meet her son's glance. Just before uttering the title of the poem, Moore's eyes met Eliza's. The poet began to read . . .

13

"A Visit from St. Nicholas"

'Twas the night before Christmas, when all through the
   house
Not a creature was stirring, not even a mouse;
The stockings were hung by the chimney with care,
In hopes that St. Nicholas soon would be there;
The children were nestled all snug in their beds,
While visions of sugar-plums danced in their heads;
And Mamma in her kerchief, and I in my cap,
Had just settled our brains for a long winter's nap;
When out on the lawn there arose such a clatter,
I sprang from the bed to see what was the matter.
Away to the window I flew like a flash,
Tore open the shutters and threw up the sash.
The moon, on the breast of the new-fallen snow,
Gave the lustre of mid-day to objects below,

When, what to my wondering eyes should appear,
But a miniature sleigh, and eight tiny reindeer,
With a little old driver, so lively and quick,
I knew in a moment it must be St. Nick.
More rapid than eagles his coursers they came,
And he whistled, and shouted, and called them by name;
"Now, *Dasher!* now, *Dancer!* now, *Prancer* and *Vixen!*
On *Comet!* on, *Cupid!* on, *Donder* and *Blitzen!*
To the top of the porch! To the top of the wall!
Now dash away! dash away! dash away all!"
As dry leaves that before the wild hurricane fly,
When they meet with an obstacle, mount to the sky;
So up to the housetop the coursers they flew,
With the sleigh full of toys, and St. Nicholas too.
And then, in a twinkling, I heard on the roof
The prancing and pawing of each little hoof.
As I drew in my head, and was turning around,
Down the chimney St. Nicholas came with a bound.
He was dressed all in fur, from his head to his foot,
And his clothes were all tarnished with ashes and soot;
A bundle of toys he had flung on his back,
And he looked like a pedlar just opening his pack.
His eyes—how they twinkled! His dimples how merry!
His cheeks were like roses, his nose like a cherry!
His droll little mouth was drawn up like a bow,
And the beard of his chin was as white as the snow;

The stump of a pipe he held tight in his teeth,
And the smoke it encircled his head like a wreath,
He had a broad face and a little round belly
That shook, when he laughed, like a bowl full of jelly.
He was chubby and plump, a right jolly old elf,
And I laughed, when I saw him, in spite of myself;
A wink of his eye and a twist of his head,
Soon gave me to know I had nothing to dread;
He spoke not a word, but went straight to his work,
And filled all the stockings; then turned with a jerk,
And laying his finger aside of his nose,
And giving a nod, up the chimney he rose;
He sprang to his sleigh, to his team gave a whistle,
And away they all flew like the down of a thistle.
But I heard him exclaim, ere he drove out of sight,
"Happy Christmas to all, and to all a good night."

14

A Christmas Triumph

HEN Moore completed his reading, he was met by total silence and faces seemingly numbed by a wintry gale. Eliza had tears in her eyes; Grandma Charity, kerchief in hand, was wiping hers. The children suddenly rushed upon their father, moved with emotion. They shouted lines of the poem . . . . ''And Mamma in her kerchief and I in my cap,'' ''away to the window I flew like a flash,'' ''Dasher, Dancer, Prancer, Vixen, Comet, Cupid, Donder, Blitzen,'' ''he looked like a pedlar just opening his pack,'' ''and giving a nod, up the chimney he rose,'' ''his belly shook like a bowl full of jelly.''

Everyone spoke at once, and the children were laughing. Charity begged her father to read the poem again, reciting, ''More rapid than eagles his coursers they came.'' Clement Clarke Moore was suddenly filled with a deep sense of exultation. The poem had been a gift for his children, and by their unanimous joyful response, he was fully convinced his gift had been well received. The poet extended his hand to receive congratulatory accolades from his servants, who also entreated the poet to give another reading of the poem.

The poet was further satisfied by the expression on Eliza's face, for her first wish was that the poem please the children, and this was more than quite evident. Even Emily, though sound asleep in her mother's arms, had a smile on her face, perhaps dreaming of sugarplums dancing in her head. Moore was happy to read his poem a second time.

With the final line, "Happy Christmas to all and to all a good night," the children tried to convince their father to give a third reading, but it was time for bed. Mama and Papa listened to their night prayers, and before long they were snoozing. The servants retired as well.

Clement and Eliza began the happy task of preparing the children's gifts, and like the words in the poem, "the stockings were hung by the chimney with care." They brimmed with Christmas gifts: imported French dolls with wigs made of real hair, and music boxes with dancing clowns and acrobats on top. These were to be gifts for the girls. For the boys, there would be hobby horses with genuine manes, toy drums, wooden replicas of King Arthur's knights, little sailboats made of oak with white silk sails. For the servants, there were clothes. The female servants received flannel gowns and hoods, warm wool nightcaps, and long stockings. The men, handsome jackets lined with rabbit fur, pouches of tobacco, and a bag of silver coins. Each servant was also given a box of special cakes made of butter and fine flour and a bag of white refined sugar—a luxury—for their tea. There were also gingerbread cakes. No servants were more loyal than those who served the poet and his family. There would also be special gifts for Grandma Charity: goose quills and special imported pink writing paper, for she loved to write to her relatives living in England.

When the Christmas chores were completed, the Moores smothered the fire in the hearth, extinguished the candles, and said goodnight to Grandma Charity. Once more they looked in upon their children. They could hear the faint motif of Cambridge Quarters coming from the downstairs parlor clock, and with the twelfth of twelve chimes, Christmas had arrived. Their thoughts turned to the Babe of Bethlehem, and they asked the little one of the Nativity to bless their own little ones.

Just before laying their heads to rest, the poet handled his nightcap, smiling, for he was reminded of the line in his poem, "And Mamma in her kerchief and I in my cap . . . ." " 'Twas the Night Before Christmas" was upon the poet's mind as he lay beside Eliza. Line after line began racing through his thoughts, until the last line of the poem swam through his mind: "Happy Christmas to all and to all a good night."

" 'Twas the Night Before Christmas" Bursts Upon the Christmas World

N 1823, the year after the creation of "A Visit from St. Nicholas," the Park Theatre in Manhattan premiered the opera *Clari,* or *Maid of Milan,* on December 11. It featured the soon to be immortal song "Home Sweet Home," and all New York was talking about the song and humming it. But Christmas was on the wing, and the city church bells, organs, pianofortes, and choirs were also singing the carols of the day: "Angels We Have Heard on High," "Hark, the Herald Angels Sing," "O Come All Ye Faithful," and "Joy to the World." Choral groups were also giving performances of George Frederick Handel's *Messiah.*

The Moore family were preparing their Christmas feast, and the poet had already exhausted himself by giving numerous family readings of " 'Twas the Night Before

Christmas,'' the line which they seemed to adopt as the title of the poem. By now, Moore knew the poem by heart. But something was afoot. Unbeknown to the Moores, the world beyond their estate was learning of ''A Visit from St. Nicholas.'' Sometime during 1823, a Miss Harriet Butler of St. Paul's Church in Troy, a very close friend of the Moore family, had been secretly allowed to read the Christmas poem by Clement's daughter Charity. What Harriet Butler read caused her to become spellbound. She entreated her young friend to allow her to print the poem in her album. ''Take care, Harriet, that Papa does not see you with the poem. I do not know my father's feelings about showing a stranger the poem,'' Charity continued. Harriet, taken aback by the word *stranger,* quickly reminded her young companion that she had been to the Chelsea estate many, many times, and that Dr. Moore and she were friends. Charity relented, justifying her position with, ''My father and your father are very close. You may take up your quill and jot down the verses for your album. But please, Harriet, do not reveal the name of the author of the poem in the album.''

On Tuesday, December 23, 1823, the Troy *Sentinel* printed a piece that soon had the townfolk buzzing, laughing, marveling, and rhapsodizing. A bit of mystery made the poem even more interesting. Clement Clarke Moore's poem appeared before the public for the first time, but the identity of the poet was not revealed. The editor of the newspaper, Orville L. Holley, prefaced the poem with this fancy explanation:

We know not to whom we are indebted for the following description of that unwearied patron of children—that homey and delightful personage of parental kindness—Santa Claus, his costume and his equipage, as he goes about visiting the firesides of this happy land, laden with Christmas bounties; but from whomsoever it may have come, we give thanks for it.—There is to our apprehension, a spirit of cordial goodness in it, a playfulness of fancy, and a benevolent alacrity to enter into the feelings and promote the simple pleasures of children, which are together charming. We hope our little patrons, both lads and lasses, will accept it as proof of our unfeigned goodwill toward them—as a token of our warmest wish that they may have many a merry Christmas; that they may long retain their beautiful relish for those unbought homebred joys, which derive their flavor from filial piety and fraternal love, and which they may be assured are the least alloyed that time can furnish them; and that they may never part with that simplicity of character, which is their own fairest ornament, and for the sake of which they have pronounced, by

Authority which none can gain say, the types of such
as shall inherit the Kingdom of heaven,

—Troy Sent'l

After the preface, the poem appeared in the *Sentinel*
with some slight changes: the title, a reversal of Moore's
punctuation in lines twenty-one and twenty-two, and a
misspelling of the name Blitzen. Moore had titled his
poem "A Visit from St. Nicholas"; the *Sentinel* titled it
"An Account of a Visit from St. Nicholas, or Santa
Claus." Moore's version of lines twenty-one and twenty-
two: "Now, Dasher! now, Dancer! now, Prancer and
Vixen! On, Comet! on Cupid! on, Donder and Blitzen!"
Sentinel's version: "Now! Dasher, now! Dancer, now!
Prancer and Vixen, On! Comet, on! Cupid, on! Donder
and *Blixen*."

We believe that Moore was to make his only comment
about the publication of his Christmas poem some time
later. Moore is believed to have commented that the
verses "were copied by a relative . . . in her album."
The word *relative* is deduced by many to mean that Harriet Butler was perhaps a very distant cousin (though it is
not known for sure), but she *had* been a frequent visitor
to the Chelsea home. What is known is that young Harriet's father was a minister, having been ordained at St.
Paul's Episcopal Church, in Troy, by Bishop Benjamin

Moore, the poet's father. But the poet must have been quietly indebted to Miss Harriet Butler for not revealing the name of the author, while he could only smile at a young daughter's slight indiscretion in sharing the Christmas ballad with a childhood chum. Moore was also charmed, no doubt, by the effusive preface. It may seem wordy, but that is the way the prose of the time was written. Flowery ornamental phrases were tolerated, if not the norm.

After 1823, the poem began its march into various forums—mostly newspapers, almanacs, broadsides, handbills, and onto the lips of children, particularly Margaret, Charity, Benjamin, Mary, Clement, Jr., and Emily. The children learned the poem by heart and would eventually realize that it was the greatest gift a parent could give. They must have taken enormous pride in knowing "A Visit from St. Nicholas" was written for them by their loving father.

16

The Family Grows—the City Grows

 OON after 1822, " 'Twas the Night Before Christmas'' would be heard by three new children presented to the poet by his Eliza: a son, William, born in 1824; a girl, Catherine, the following year; and in 1827, the third addition, Maria Theresa, to become known as Terry. This brought the Moore brood to a final total of nine children.

These years also brought changes and innovations to Manhattan. With the opening of the Erie Canal in 1825, the foghorns from the Hudson River commerce became incessant. The poet's daily journeys into lower Manhattan to teach at Trinity brought him into a city where mud streets were being paved with cobblestone, a greater number of lamps were lighting the city streets by night, most New York children were attending city

THE HUDSON RIVER, VIEWING NEW YORK, 1825

schools, and more constables and night watchmen were noticeable. The city, however, was still without a sewer system or official fire and police departments.

The poet could see why his property taxes were almost $20,000 a year—not high for a man who had everything: a loving spouse whom he worshiped, beautiful children, a great deal of property, influential friends. Clement Clarke Moore was very grateful and enjoyed sharing his riches; it was the practice of many a beggar to frequent the Chelsea homestead for food and money, and there were close friends who needed loans and assistance in their endeavors. The poet of Christmas Eve followed the dicta ''To him that is given much, much is expected in return," and "Bread upon the waters multiples a hundredfold." While he was a great benefactor to his parish churches, Moore particularly enjoyed giving anonymously. Many a person was the recipient of the poet's goodness without ever knowing the giver.

It is not surprising that anonymous generosity is a major theme of his Christmas ballad. It is only when the children are "snug in their beds," when all life is quiet in sleep, "not a creature was stirring not even a mouse," that St. Nicholas appears, as if a leprechaun. But unlike the Irish gnomes that hide their gold, St. Nick comes bearing gifts, filling all the stockings "hung by the chimney with care."

17

Ill Winds Strike Chelsea

 N 1828 Emily died—the child who loved to daydream of dancing sugarplums, who loved to recite the Christmas ballad to her friends. Her death brought Clement Clarke Moore to a low point in his life, and peace was not his for years to come.

As the poet was beginning to rise from this deep grief, comforted in the arms of his lifelong companion, those loving arms would fall still. On April 4, 1830, Eliza's heart fell silent. She was thirty-six years old when death came. Moore was almost inconsolable. The words of his youngest child, Maria Theresa, as the child gazed upon her mother's still face, were indelible in his mind: "Mama won't speak to me anymore, she is gone to a better place." Her heart just gave out, for she died of what was termed a "disordered frame." She had been the most meaningful thing in the poet's existence. She had replaced his father, Benjamin, and his mother, Charity, as his mentor. Charity was to write to a relative in England that Eliza was "the most patient, uncomplaining being. A companion to his heart."

For months after her death, Eliza's spirit was with Moore in many ways: the way she used her hands, her delicate mannerisms, the sway of her gait, her loving countenance as she conversed with him about the children, her sighs of concern when he worked too hard, her voice, like music from a harp. These characteristics were to be painfully witnessed in the voices and gestures of the children, who seemed to move closer to their father, as if trying to protect him. As he looked down upon their faces of love and innocence, Eliza's face melted through his thoughts, for each child bore some resemblance to her. So often as he listened to their night prayers, took their hands, shared their joys and sorrows, his years with Eliza raced through his thoughts: the birth of each child, the wonderful Christmas times together, her composure under stress, the way she laughed when he shared a humorous tale. He was hearing her and seeing her in their children. Indeed, like a church bell that peals, its echo reverberating into the breezes to be savored, Eliza Moore had thoroughly bequeathed her image to their children. It was an immortal and beautiful legacy that would warm Clement's spirit for the remainder of his life.

18

Still a Christmas Secret

HE year 1830 was the most trying year of Moore's life. Soon after his beloved wife's death, Charity Elizabeth, his second oldest child, fell ill with tuberculosis. In August, Moore brought her to Saratoga Springs, hoping that the change of air would improve her health. He wrote, his heart full of grief and fear, to his mother: "We must, of course, be governed by wind and weather, and other circumstances. I am a burnt child; I dread the fire. What I have seen result from a beginning smaller, in appearance, than that which is now before me, keeps my mind in a state of constant alarm. I repine not at the ways of Providence, and am ready to submit to whatever may be imposed upon me; but I trust and pray that my heart may not again be rent.''

His prayers were not to be answered. Within the shadows of Christmas, on December 14, 1830, Charity Elizabeth died. She was barely fourteen.

Moore, heartbroken and near despair, threw himself into those activities he knew would begin to heal his soul: his work, his faith, his family, and the Christmas poem that had brought so much joy to his loved ones, present and absent. His little ballad was now increasingly spreading its happy message in a wider and wider circle.

The first known illustrations of "An Account of a Visit from St. Nicholas, or Santa Claus," as designed by illustrator Myron King, depicting St. Nicholas in a sleigh drawn by his reindeer, appeared as a broadside through the office of the Troy *Sentinel,* the newspaper that was the first to break the Christmas poem to the world. This second time around, the *Sentinel* used Moore's punctuation and corrected its other mistake, changing "Blixen" to its proper "Blitzen." Other newspapers also ran the poem, including the first-known abridgment of the poem by a Philadelphia publisher—Annals of Philadelphia—that compiled a collection of Philadelphia lore. The copy reported to its Germantown readers that St. Nicholas was known also as "Christkind" to the English and "Belsnickel" to the Germans. Still, with each passing Christmas and the many, many publications of the poem, the demand to name its author mounted. In the previous year, the editor of the Troy *Sentinel,* Orville Holley, wrote in his Christmas edition that the author ''belonged by birth and residence to the City of New York, and that he is a gentleman of more merit as a scholar and writer than many of more pretensions.''

In the early 1830s, Moore was busy teaching at the newly opened General Theological Seminary, just a stone's throw from his front door. When he was not busy raising his children and managing his numerous real estate holdings, he was extending hospitality to his many social acquaintances—bankers, former mayors, literary friends, legal and ecclesiastical notables of the hour. The big house was homey and always lively with music, as Moore often joined friends, performing works by Scarlatti and Vivaldi on his violin. As a professor who was often called Dr. Moore, he played host to many of his students, allowing them into his home for tea and talk. These years were also busy with his new project, the erecting of a new Episcopal church to be known as St. Peter's. Aside from donating the land, as he had done with the General Theological Seminary, the poet also raised a great deal of money for the structure, including finding funds for an organ worth an unheard-of sum of $5,000. The organ may still be seen at St. Peter's today.

For almost fourteen years, Moore had kept a copy of the Troy *Sentinel*'s first publication of his poem, and had dozens of additional copies from newspapers, almanacs, and broadsides. Each tried to outdo the other, some implying that they would reveal the author, though they didn't actually know the creator of the Christmas verse. The poet saw greed in their motives, for any implication of knowing the author of " 'Twas the Night Before Christmas" was bound to sell more papers. Moore would receive no royalties for his work, for copyright laws had not yet been established. In essence, he had made a Christmas gift to the world of his poem.

The poet's children were happy to comply with their father's wish for secrecy, though Grandma Charity, still alert and wise in her nineties, began to wonder aloud about the wisdom of his secrecy regarding the masterpiece. She guessed that sooner or later some person would stake a claim to "A Visit From St. Nicholas."

19

A Name Above " 'Twas the Night Before Christmas"

ITTING before the same fireside where George Washington had given his word to Mary Stillwell Clarke that the Continental soldiers would cease making a nuisance of themselves, and where Moore had first read the immortal verses of ''A Visit from St. Nicholas,'' the poet agonized about whether he should break his silence. The hearth held memories so dear to his heart, memories made more poignant because his beloved Eliza was gone. He looked at her empty chair, unused since her death, wool yarn she was working with when suddenly taken ill still upon it. The chair was close to the fireplace, for she had complained of the cold.

Everything had remained as Eliza left it. The thought of Emily and Charity, as little babies, crawling toward its

BROADWAY LOOKING SOUTH FROM ST. PAUL'S IN 1835

warmth, made Moore smile, for he could see them all and hear their voices.

Grandma Charity's hand touching his shoulder showed signs of frailness in 1837. Before both of them was a letter from editor and friend Charles Genno Hoffmann, of *The New York Book of Poetry,* thanking Moore for his letter. He and the publisher knew of his poem and honored his request for secrecy, but were now most pleased and privileged to be the first in bringing the poem to the public with the name of its author. The anthology contained other poems, but this publication finally announced to the world that " 'Twas the Night Before Christmas" had been written by Moore and by Moore alone. Grandma Charity was beaming with pride, and the children—Margaret, all grown up and married to a doctor; Benjamin, a young man of nineteen; Mary, at present eighteen years; Clement, Jr., seventeen; William, Catherine, and Maria Theresa, still very young—all knew that far too many years had passed with the absence of an author's name to the poem. At last, and for all time, " 'Twas the Night Before Christmas" would have a name before its verses—the name of Clement Clarke Moore.

20

A Dream's Swan Song

RANDMA Charity had seen her son's Christmas ballad come to prominence and public acknowledgment. She had been a beacon to her son and grandchildren. In 1838, at the age of ninety-one, this wonderful woman, who had stayed by her son's side all her life, gave up her spirit. Through her the world learned that the night of the first Christmas reading of her son's poem was very, very special to her son, her granddaughters, and grandsons. Of Christmas Eve of 1822, she once wrote: ''There does not appear to have been another like the Christmas Eve when Margaret, Charity, Benjamin, Mary, Clement, and Emily first heard their 'dear father' introduce St. Nicholas at Chelsea House.'' The passing of Grandma Charity Clarke Moore left an emptiness at Chelsea Homestead that was destined never to be filled.

With the knowledge that Clement Clarke Moore was

the author of " 'Twas the Night Before Christmas," requests began coming in to Chelsea for personal, handwritten copies of the poem. Though there are only two known handwritten copies by the poet, somewhere in the world other copies may exist, for Moore handwrote the poem to his friends on quality parchment that was capable of withstanding the rigors of time. In 1840, "A Visit from St. Nicholas" appeared in Harper Brothers' *Selections from the Americans Poets*. This was important because it gave the Christmas poem great literary prestige. The great march of the poem was in full swing, and with it, information about its author appeared in every print medium available and was copied with quills by schoolchildren and grown-ups alike.

In 1844, Moore issued his own 216-page book of his poems. In this book, a preface by the author is addressed to "My Dear Children," and—on pages 124 to 127—one finds the immortal Christmas masterpiece. Privately published, the author was swamped with requests for copies. On January 2, 1845, the *New York Daily Mirror* ran parts of the poem, altering " 'Twas the Night Before Christmas" to " 'Twas the Night Before New Year's," and closing with "Happy New Year to all and to all a Goodnight."

April 13 brought the death of daughter Margaret, never really strong. Moore attempted to take her death in stride. It was also the year Moore's son William graduated from Columbia College. His degree was conferred by the president of Columbia, Nathaniel Fish Moore, a cousin of the Moore family.

If the poet's Christmas ballad could withstand time, Chelsea could not. The railroad had arrived, and the tranquility of Chelsea Homestead began to fade. From his large window, Moore observed steel tracks being laid across his property. With the railroad would come the massive westside build-up of Manhattan and the slow death of Chelsea. The poet was powerless, for the good of the city outweighed individual rights. Before long came breweries, slaughterhouses, and glue factories. The sycamores, elms, oaks, and chestnuts were lost to progress.

The handsome face of the poet began to succumb to age, and his hairline began receding, but those knowing

GENERAL THEOLOGICAL SEMINARY IN 1846

and peaceful eyes never lost their wistful twinkle. With the children gone or into their own lives or about to find their own way, the poet was resigned to all the changes. One happy note in 1848 was Mary, stepping up to the altar to marry Margaret's widower.

Wise business practices and astute business friends enabled Moore to have much of his Chelsea property developed the way he wished. A clause as to all future development has held for more than a century, right up to today. As written by Moore: "No building can be erected for any purpose which will make the neighborhood disagreeable, and it becoming a favorite place of residence."

Entrusting the developing of Chelsea to an artisan friend named Don Alonzo Cushman, Moore saw that the neighborhood houses were built in the Greek Revival style. These houses of red brick and sloping roofs were fronted with cast-iron gates, wreaths encircling small attic windows, areaway fences, and iron stoop railings. To this day, Chelsea is considered prized property and one of the best Manhattan neighborhoods in which to raise a family, as the poet had intended. Indeed, Clement Clarke Moore was a man of wisdom.

21

Farewell to Home and Hearth

HE poet of Christmas Eve had not lost the spring in his step; he continued to teach young seminarians their Greek and Oriental literature. His young charges and his peers always seemed struck by the enormous contrast between the scholar Moore and the poet Moore, who could compose the most beloved Christmas poem in the English language. In 1848, that poem would be treated to its most sumptuous setting when it enjoyed its first complete illustration, the distinction belonging to a wood engraver named T. C. Boyd. The publisher, Henry M. Onderdonck, was a friend of the poet. This edition marks the first time the poem was published alone in book form. Six illustrations accompanied the text. Boyd's art gives today's reader a glimpse of New York at the time of the poet. Among the illustrations are Santa in a Russian hat and very tiny sleigh, with seven, instead of eight, reindeer (he left out Dancer). Both Santa Claus and the name St. Nicholas are used. Moore had to be tickled pink by the book and with it, his reputation as a professor was quickly overshadowed by that as a Christmas poet.

With time spinning into the mid-nineteenth century, there was talk of telephones, refrigeration, flying machines, sewing machines. A sewer system had become a reality for Manhattan (1850), and an official fire department as well as a police department was also in place. The poet could only wonder what was next. Hamilton Fish was governor of New York; Caleb S. Woodhull was mayor of New York City; Millard Fillmore was President of the Untied States. Henry Clay opened the great debate on slavery, warning the South against secession from the Union; Turkey would soon declare war on Russia in what would become the Crimean War.

New things were happening or had occurred regarding Christmas. Charles Dickens had written *A Christmas Carol* in 1843. The greatest Christmas carol, ''Silent Night,'' written in 1818, was beginning to find its way to the New World, even while the music world of Europe was searching for the true authors of the carol. Attributing the work to both Mozart and Haydn, they would soon learn that a Catholic priest named Father Joseph

Mohr, and Franz Xavier Gruber, a schoolteacher, were its true creators. The Christmas card was becoming a tradition, established in England in 1842; the Christmas tree was also becoming a beloved Yuletide symbol, having been brought to England by Prince Albert from his homeland, Germany. The long reign of his wife and queen, Victoria of England, was giving rise to the expression "Victorian Christmas," with balls, beaver hats, snowy coaches, plum puddings, and charity toward the poor.

In 1851, Clement Clarke Moore retired from teaching, taking the title of professor emeritus. The poet's life was now his children and his acts of philanthropy. Near the end of his life, his beloved Chelsea home was swallowed up and torn down in the name of progress. Streets and avenues claimed the place where his home once stood, as dictated by a city planning commission in 1811.

Chelsea Homestead, where the Moore children were born and where some died, where his Eliza and Charity Moore had spent their lives, where all had laughed and cried and loved, and where " 'Twas the Night Before Christmas" was born, was gone forever.

22

Many Years Ago

 LEMENT Clarke Moore grew into old age gracefully, an elderly gentleman of leisure. Born during a revolution, the final years of his life came when the country he loved so much was again involved in a conflict—the Civil War. Still the poet gave occasional talks at the General Theological Seminary and attended church almost every morning. Retirement suited him well.

On March 13, 1862, at the request of a friend, for the very last of many times, the poet wrote the fifty-six lines that had brought him Christmas immortality. After writing the poem, he signed his customary signature, added the date, and closed with, ''originally written many years ago.'' The poet was eighty-three years of age. Living at a townhouse in the city, he would leave the place of his birth forever on June 1, 1863, setting sail by night up Long Island Sound, bound for Newport, Rhode Island, and a visit with his daughter Mary.

On July 10, a peaceful day and not too hot, the poet's eyes fell upon his sons and daughters. Lifting his frail head, the poet's wistful, serene smile found his loved ones. He wanted to tell them not to weep. The smile on his face was still there as the light of life left his eyes.

Clement Clarke Moore wanted to be remembered for trying to be a good father, a kind man who had a hand in the development of young minds, minds that would teach people the gospel of love and charity to all. But the world would not remember him for his many good works. The world would remember Clement Clarke Moore for '' 'Twas the Night Before Christmas.''

 LEMENT Clarke Moore's remains reposed at St. Luke's churchyard, not far from his beloved Chelsea, until 1890, when the property was sold. The Christmas poet's remains were interred at Trinity Cemetery of the Church of Intercession, at One-hundred-fifty-fifth Street, New York City. Annually at Christmastide and on Christmas Eve, the gravesite is the scene of numerous recitations of his beloved '' 'Twas the Night Before Christmas,'' accompanied by candlelight ceremonies and the singing of carols.

Significant Dates

1609: John Moor, sailing into New York Harbor on the vessel *Half Moon*, becomes the first of Clement Clarke Moore's family to settle in the New World.

1647: Another ancestor, the Reverend John Moore, settles in Middleburg, afterwards called Newtown and now Elmhurst.

1654: The Reverend John Moore becomes friendly with the Indians and is given property, which his children inherit.

1692: Thomas Clarke, Clement Clarke Moore's grandfather, is born on August 11.

1745: Captain Thomas Clarke marries the vivacious Mary Stillwell, of notable English parentage.

1747:   Charity Clarke, Clement Clarke Moore's mother, is born, the eldest of five children.

1748:   Benjamin Moore, Clement Clarke Moore's father, is born on October 5.

1768:   Benjamin Moore graduates from King's College (now Columbia University) at age seventeen.

1771:   Benjamin Moore travels to England, where he is ordained a deacon, then a priest.

1775:   Bishop Benjamin Moore becomes president of Columbia University.

1776:   Captain Thomas Clarke dies at age eighty-five, after lingering near death for two years, from burns due to a fire.

1778:   Benjamin Moore marries Charity Clarke on April 30, at Trinity Church.

1779:   Clement Clarke Moore, only child of Benjamin and Charity Moore, is born on July 15.

1794:   Catherine Elizabeth Taylor, Clement Clarke Moore's wife, is born.

1798:   Clement Clark Moore graduates from Columbia University at nineteen.

1801:   Clement Clarke Moore receives his master's degree from Columbia University. Begins his *Lexicon on the Hebrew Language*, in two volumes.

1804: Bishop Benjamin Moore gives the last rites to Alexander Hamilton.

1809: Clement Clarke Moore's *Lexicon on the Hebrew Language* is published, with the express hope that it might aid others to aquire a knowledge of Hebrew. Benjamin Moore deeds his estate to his son. Washington Irving writes his *Knickerbocker's History of New York*.

1811: Benjamin Moore becomes paralyzed.

1813: Clement Clarke Moore marries Catherine Elizabeth Taylor on November 20, at Varick Street.

1815: Margaret Moore is born on June 6, the first of nine children.

1816: Charity Elizabeth Moore, is born September 11. Bishop Benjamin Moore dies at the age of sixty-eight.

1818: Benjamin Moore is born.

1819: Mary Moore is born.

1820: Clement, Jr., is born.

1821: "A New Year's Present to the Little Ones from Five to Twelve" is published.

1822: Emily Moore is born. Clement Clarke Moore writes his famous poem "A Visit from St. Nicholas," which becomes popularly known by the poem's first line, " 'Twas the Night Before Christmas."

1823: Clement Clarke Moore's famous poem is published anonymously on December 23, under the title "An Account of a Visit from St. Nicholas" in the Troy *Sentinel*, an upstate New York newspaper.

1824: William Moore is born.

1825: Catherine is born. The Erie Canal opens.

1827: Maria Theresa is born.

1828: Emily Moore dies at age six.

1830: Catherine Elizabeth Taylor Moore dies on April 4, at thirty-six. Her daughter Charity Elizabeth Moore dies on December 14, at age fourteen.

1835: Margaret Elliot Moore marries Dr. Doughty Ogden on October 1.

1837: Clement Clarke Moore reveals his authorship in an anthology of poems entitled *The New York Book of Poetry*, acknowledging his famous poem, "A Visit from St. Nicholas."

1838: The *Troy Budget* acknowledges Clement Clarke Moore as the author of the poem "A Visit from St. Nicholas," December 23. Grandma Charity Moore dies at the age of ninety-one at Chelsea House.

1845: Margaret Moore dies on April 13. William Moore graduates from Columbia University.

1848: Mary Moore marries her sister Margaret's widower, Dr. Doughty Ogden. First complete illustrations by T. C. Boyd of the beloved Christmas poem in English language.

1851: Clement Clarke Moore retires from teaching.

1854: All of Clement Clarke Moore's Chelsea homestead gone.

1862: Clement Clarke Moore dies on July 10, at Newport, Rhode Island, at the age of eighty-four. He is buried at St. Luke's Church on Hudson Street.

1890: The poet's body is interred at Holy Trinity Cemetery at One-hundred-fifty-fifth Street and Broadway in upper Manhattan after the St. Luke's property is sold.

'Twas the night before Christmas, when all through
    the house
Not a creature was stirring, not even a mouse;
The stockings were hung by the chimney with care,
In hopes that St. Nicholas soon would be there;
The children were nestled all snug in their beds,
While visions of sugar-plums danced in their heads;
And mamma in her 'kerchief, and I in my cap,
Had just settled our brains for a long winter's nap;
When out on the lawn there arose such a clatter,
I sprang from the bed to see what what was the matter.
Away to the window I flew like a flash,
Tore open the shutters and threw up the sash.
The moon, on the breast of the new-fallen snow,
Gave the lustre of mid-day to objects below,
When, what to my wondering eyes should appear,
But a miniature sleigh, and eight tiny rein-deer,
With a little old driver, so lively and quick,
I knew in a moment it must be St. Nick.
More rapid than eagles his coursers they came,
And he whistled, and shouted, and called them by name;
"Now, Dasher! now, Dancer! now, Prancer and Vixen!
On, Comet! on, Cupid! on, Donder and Blitzen!
To the top of the porch! to the top of the wall!
Now dash away! dash away! dash away all!"

As dry leaves that before the wild hurricane fly,
When they meet with an obstacle, mount to the sky;
So up to the house-top the coursers they flew,
With the sleigh full of Toys, and St. Nicholas too.
And then, in a twinkling, I heard on the roof
The prancing and pawing of each little hoof —
As I drew in my head, and was turning around,
Down the chimney St. Nicholas came with a bound.
He was dressed all in fur, from his head to his foot,
And his clothes were all tarnished with ashes and soot;
A bundle of Toys he had flung on his back,
And he look'd like a pedlar just opening his pack.
His eyes — how they twinkled! his dimples how merry!
His cheeks were like roses, his nose like a cherry!
His droll little mouth was drawn up like a bow,
And the beard of his chin was as white as the snow;
The stump of a pipe he held tight in his teeth,
And the smoke it encircled his head like a wreath;
He had a broad face and a little round belly
That shook, when he laughed, like a bowl full of jelly.
He was chubby and plump, a right jolly old elf,
And I laughed, when I saw him, in spite of myself;
A wink of his eye and a twist of his head,
Soon gave me to know I had nothing to dread;

He spoke not a word, but went straight to his work,
And fill'd all the stockings; then turned with a jerk,
And laying his finger aside of his nose,
And giving a nod, up the chimney he rose;
He sprang to his sleigh, to his team gave a whistle,
And away they all flew like the down of a thistle.
But I heard him exclaim, ere he drove out of sight,
" Happy Christmas to all, and to all a good night."

Clement C. Moore,
1862, March 13th originally written
many years ago.

"Visit from St. Nicholas" manuscript poem by Clement Clarke
Moore. Courtesy of The New-York Historical Society, N.Y.C.